TWO MAGPIES BAKERY

Stories and Recipes from
the Heart of East Anglia

Rebecca Bishop

Photography by India Hobson

CONTENTS

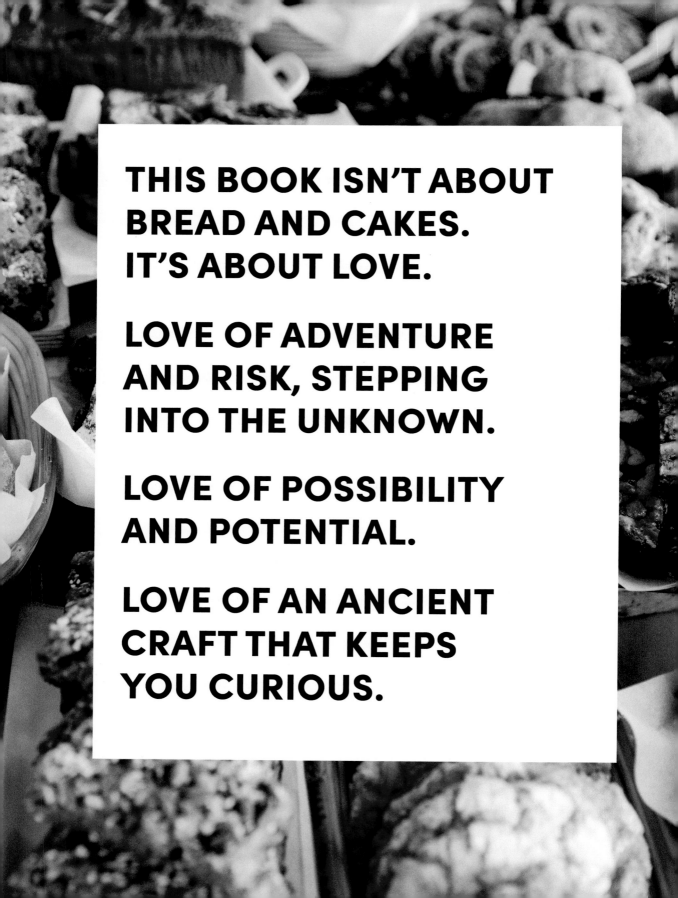

THIS BOOK ISN'T ABOUT
BREAD AND CAKES.
IT'S ABOUT LOVE.

LOVE OF ADVENTURE
AND RISK, STEPPING
INTO THE UNKNOWN.

LOVE OF POSSIBILITY
AND POTENTIAL.

LOVE OF AN ANCIENT
CRAFT THAT KEEPS
YOU CURIOUS.

I don't come from a family of bakers, nor did I learn to whip up a cake at my mother's knee. After attending boarding school with weekly 'domestic science' lessons that still make me shudder, I married in my early twenties and with three young children, my home became my outlet for creativity and resourcefulness. I've always been a practical person, so I knitted, sewed, fixed up houses, grew vegetables, pickled, preserved and worked my way through some wonderful culinary classics – Jane Grigson, Constance Spry and Elizabeth David to name a few.

Divorce, then an art degree, followed by teacher training developed my creativity and resilience further, but it was in my kitchen where I relaxed and lost myself in daydreams, flavours, flour, butter and sugar. In 2009, I read a magazine article about sourdough bread and started making it – loads of it, more than I could give to friends, family, colleagues at work and the kids I was teaching. It was clogging up my kitchen, filling up my brain and my recipe collection was threatening to take over the house!

Around this time, I fell in love with a man who was as obsessed with food as I was and together we baked and dreamed up crazy plans for a new start. Inspired by a visit to the open-plan Town Mill Bakery in Lyme Regis, we started searching for a space that would engage customers with the sights, sounds and smells of baking, creating delicious food from quality raw ingredients while giving us the opportunity to work with a team of like-minded people.

My children had flown the nest and with the whole of the UK as a potential option, research trips were enjoyed in far-flung places, such as the Isle of Skye and Berwick-upon-Tweed. Common sense eventually prevailed and even without any business experience, I knew that bakeries need customers to succeed – and so an algorithm (referred to as the 'rule of three') was fine-tuned to focus on prosperous towns with a quality butcher, greengrocer but, crucially, no bakery.

In April 2012, after many days on the road, we visited Southwold on the Suffolk coast – a place identified through Google Maps as conforming to the 'rule of three'. I had visited this sleepy corner of England years before and remembered its unspoilt charms. Reminiscent of a 1950s picture postcard, its appeal is enduring and quintessentially British. Generations of families return year after year to enjoy trips up the lighthouse, a walk to the end of the pier, beach-hut picnics, crabbing at the harbour or taking the rowing boat to Walberswick across the estuary. Southwold is small enough to walk around in one day but within easy reach of undeveloped coastline and heathlands beneath vast East Anglian skies.

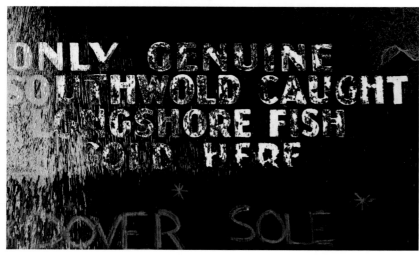

Our property enquiries were met with enthusiasm but also a sharp intake of breath and shake of the head. Undeterred and prepared for the long game, we were hailed by a glamorous older lady as we headed back to the car. A local councillor with her ear to the ground, she'd 'heard' that number 88, an Edwardian glass-fronted shop that had seen better days, was coming onto the market. It was a long way from the open-plan bakery of our dreams – small and narrow with just a loo and rusty sink in a rotting lean-to at the back – but with a small flat above, planning permission already in place to extend over the overgrown yard and rose-tinted glasses firmly in place, the rest, as they say, is history.

By September I had left my job, sold my house and ploughed my life savings into the project. Builders, architects and shop fitters came together quickly to construct our bakery at the rear with an open viewing window onto the shop so we could chat to customers while we worked. Our plan was to be open by Easter 2013, so our days (and sleepless nights) quickly filled with Tetris-style floor plans, eBay searches for monstrously expensive equipment, building regulations and employment law. Edited 'highlights' include persuading UK power networks to squeeze a little more juice from the town's three-phase electricity supply, and a change-of-use planning application, which saw us embroiled in a class action against a well-known coffee chain. We knew we had chosen a very special place when half of Southwold descended on Lowestoft town hall to lobby on our behalf!

With the opening date fast approaching, we needed a name and Two Magpies was suggested. Amongst friends and family, I'm known for my habit of collecting – scribbled notes on scraps of paper, sketches and recipes scrawled in many, many battered notebooks. I designed our logo, hired a sign writer to paint our name above the door and penned the 'baked with joy' by-line for our paperwork and receipts – a nod to the traditional Magpie rhyme. The shop and café were designed to reflect the form and function of a working bakery with simple lines and natural materials. Whitewashed Douglas fir wraps the counters and shelves, wooden shingles hang from the wall in shades of grey and the tables are made for sharing.

At 7 am on Good Friday 2013, the blinds were raised to a queue stretching down the street – a moment both terrifying and exhilarating in equal measure. Four weeks behind schedule and massively over budget, there had been no time for test bakes and we got through that busy holiday weekend on adrenalin and coffee.

My memories of the early days of the bakery are largely sleep deprivation, exhaustion, mistakes, mistakes and more mistakes. I knew nothing about hospitality and manufacturing, recruiting and managing people or running a business. Suffice to say, it was incredibly stressful – the bakery felt like an insatiable beast eating us up and spitting us out. Days were relentless – baking all night and long into the next day, trying to sleep in the afternoon in the flat above the bakery, then starting all over again at 9 pm.

My then-husband and I parted company only 18 months into the business and the time that followed – coping with heartbreak, divorce and the demands of the bakery – was tough. We were now down to just one baker, so a move from the pastry section to working the bread shift was essential. I still remember my first solo bake – letting myself into the silent bakery, the buzz of fluorescent tubes blinking into life. After having a stern word with myself, I took a deep breath and got to work. However challenging the night ahead was, I was determined to appear confident and calm when the pastry shift arrived at 4 am.

With the support of our team, community and fellow baker Martha from Forge Bakehouse, I didn't just survive the challenges of running the business singlehandedly, they actually became the catalyst for much-needed change as we eventually moved away from night shifts, making the business a more robust and sustainable place to work.

Just like any home baker, we've had our fair share of dramas along the way – hilarious in hindsight but stressful at the time – our cold prover accidentally switching to hot, hours before it was needed or noticed, resulting in the pungent overfermentation of Stilton bread that lingered for weeks. Or the time our mixer broke down and the Crown Hotel kitchen next door kindly let us use theirs – but because it was much smaller than ours, multiple mixes were required and we spent the small hours shuttling the dough back and forth in the dark.

Fast forward five years and with a new business partner, Steve Magnall, we opened our second Suffolk site in nearby Aldeburgh – Southwold's grown-up, streetwise cousin. Its wide high street affords glimpses of the sea between art galleries, bookshops and independent fashion shops.

Making enough bread and cakes to satisfy hungry customers requires silly-size ovens, mixers and refrigeration. After five years of increasingly cramped conditions in Southwold, we took the plunge to expand the bakery, taking on the empty shell of an ex-small supermarket a few miles down the road in Darsham. Not only did this give us the space

to bake for more shops (Norwich, then Blakeney and Holt in North Norfolk, before returning to our roots in Woodbridge, Suffolk) and increase our team of bakers and pastry chefs – it also allowed me to realise the dream of opening a baking school to share my skills and passion for Real Bread.

As the business has grown, we've built a strong and loyal team – from senior managers to weekend pot washers – who are not only wonderful at what they do but have also enabled me to have the time to write this book. Over the years I've had countless customers wanting to find out how we do what we do, so it's a delight to be able to share some of our best-loved recipes, baking stories and tips and techniques.

Our ethos

Just as Two Magpies has grown over the last decade, so has the nation's appetite for real food, provenance and traceability. Baking from scratch and working with small local suppliers who share our ethos is key to everything we do. We buy most of our flour from the historic Marriage's Millers in Essex, beans and pulses from Hodmedod's in Brampton, Suffolk pork from Clarke's of Bramfield, cheese and buttermilk for our soda bread from award-winning Fen Farm Dairy, beer from the Adnams brewery in Southwold and organic rye flour from Maple Farm, Kelsale. We're proud of what we do and want the world to see how we do it. Customers delight in watching our pastry chefs skilfully icing a cake, the bakers hand-moulding bread or stretching pizza dough. We believe these skills deserve to be celebrated and we hope that we're an inspiration to home bakers.

Southwold

One of the things that visitors and locals alike love is the way Southwold transforms itself through the seasons of the year.

During the winter months, the town is quiet as I walk briskly up the high street, stopping to pick up a coffee at the bakery and then down the Nelson steps to the beach: windswept and wild. Spectacular winter sunsets stop you in your tracks. The lighthouse winking against a darkening sky streaked pink and orange and the silhouettes of starling murmurations hang over the reedbeds. As daylight fades, I head to the warmth of the bakery with cold hands and glowing cheeks, ready to indulge in hot chocolate and cake.

Our location means we get to know our customers well. Some we see many times a day for a coffee fix, others pop in during the week for a loaf of bread and a treat. Holiday homeowners are welcomed back as long-lost friends and those new to Southwold become 'regulars' even during a short holiday.

Easter is the start of the holiday season and we're all hoping for sunshine and blue skies. As the days lengthen, the dunes are bright with yellow gorse, their coconut scent hanging heavy in the air. A rainbow of freshly painted beach huts stands to attention as the town brushes itself off, preparing for another year. The bakery is busy during the week with the ebb and flow of locals and busier still at the weekends with day trippers – a pattern we've come to know and understand.

Visitor numbers increase as the temperature rises. School holiday madness is soon upon us. In the morning, children wait patiently in the queue, clutching the family wish list, before staggering home, bags bulging with freshly baked croissants and warm bread. Holiday-makers enjoy leisurely breakfasts and deliberate over picnic necessities and mid-afternoon treats. In this part of the world, an early morning swim is de rigueur and we're used to serving coffee and croissants to customers sporting robes over their 'swimmers'. The town resonates with life and laughter as the resident population swells. Just walking down the high street can prove challenging and the bakery is at full capacity – it's standing room only!

We love our summer visitors but there's a collective sigh of relief at the start of September as the town re-groups, compares notes and welcomes those looking for a little peace and solitude. The Aldeburgh Food & Drink Festival, set in the grounds of beautiful Snape Maltings, is an opportunity to chat to regular customers at our stand, meet other suppliers and shout about what we do with workshops and demos. During November, we welcome some famous faces to the bakery during Southwold Literary Festival and bake buns with the local school children for St Edmund's Day. As the year draws to a close, the smell of Christmas puddings steaming drifts through the bakery and we dust off our mince pie tally chart and iced gingerbread snowflakes to hang in the shop window. Orders for Christmas bread and baked treats are carefully noted as we plan how we'll tackle the biggest bake of the year – this requires some epic shifts from our heroic bakers!

The Suffolk coast is a special place – and if you know, you know. Nostalgia is a strong pull and many of our customers, jaded from urban noise and bright lights, have returned to where their early years were spent crunching over shingle beaches, freewheeling down country lanes and learning to swim in the brown waters of the North Sea. In fact, we find they're positively evangelical about it! Over the last twenty years, the returnees have been joined by zealous converts, spry retirees and second homers who realised they were onto something good. The recent rise in staycations has meant that the Suffolk and Norfolk coast has experienced a massive rise in visitor numbers rediscovering the simple pleasures of sprawling family picnics, the sound of curlews on the salt marshes, brightly painted beach huts, picture-postcard seaside towns and those big, big skies.

Getting started

Reading recipe books cover to cover is how I relax. I tend to cook from memory, using the concept or the ingredients of a recipe rather than slavishly following it word for word. With baking, however, scientific precision is key to consistent results, so this approach doesn't work with bread and pastry.

Use this collection of recipes as a foundation to inspire, guide and develop your baker's intuition – it takes time and practice to master a new skill, so don't be too hard on yourself and constantly compare your bakes with those on social media or in recipe books.

Check your ingredients list regularly as you progress – did you miss anything out? Some mistakes result in happy accidents – I remember finding some melted butter in the microwave hours after a chocolate cake had been consumed and realising the cake was delicious without it!

Consider the physicality of the baking process. While your hands are busy performing a skilled set of manoeuvres, your mind is free to wander and consider the creative potential of your ingredients. Frustrations are always going to occur, but trial and error are as much a part of being a baker as enjoying the fruits of your labour. Think of baking as a blank canvas for your creativity. Grasp the basics of the processes and you'll soon find yourself daydreaming about the potential you've unlocked!

The three times rule

After many over-ambitious disasters, I always follow my three times rule, starting with a base recipe and then moving sideways in a documented series of trials – changing the flour, spice or flavour, the shape or cooking method, decoration or presentation. Surprises lead to innovation and fresh ideas. Mistakes inform us and enable us to move forwards.

1/ **The first time,** just hope for something that tastes OK. Nothing more. Choose an occasion when you're under no pressure to succeed – just relax and enjoy the process. When you've finished, take a few minutes to reflect on the outcome, jot down what you'll change next time and then feed it to hungry children or kindly work colleagues – they won't turn down free food no matter how ugly or wonky it is!

2/ **The second time,** make sure you read all the parts you skipped last time (yes, we've all done it) and apply your growing knowledge to the method – adapting your technique to achieve the consistency required, tweaking the flavour or adjusting the bake time and oven heat. Again, make a note of the outcome – this will take you closer to the result you're after.

3/ **By the third time,** the recipe will be your own – a friend, not a mystery. With growing confidence and understanding, you'll be able to adapt and switch flavours, increase or decrease quantities and change the style and decoration to suit. Feel proud of what you have accomplished. Apply the three times rule to every new recipe and you'll never feel a failure again.

Equipment

YOUR OVEN

Every oven is different, so use timings as a guide. When I'm trialling a recipe, I set the timer for as little as a few minutes so I can monitor and assess the product by smell, touch and sight as it bakes. Ideally, your oven should heat up to at least 240°C/220°C fan/gas 9 and be big enough to hold your Dutch oven. Turn it into a proving cabinet on cooler days by turning on for 1 minute on a low setting, then turn off, just leaving the light on. The energy from the light bulb should maintain your dough temperature at 26°C.

STAND MIXER

I prefer to make bread by hand. It's not nearly as physically demanding as most people think and touching the dough, observing it and feeling the texture as it develops have made me a better baker. You may also find that stiffer doughs get stuck on the dough hook so don't develop gluten effectively and mixers create friction, heating up your dough (particularly a stiff one), which can lead to overproving in summer. However, some very wet doughs, such as focaccia or ciabatta, are easier to manage in a mixer. It's a different matter, however, when it comes to making cakes and pastries! Beating cake batter until it's light and fluffy or meringues to stiff peaks is no mean feat, so, if you have access to one, I suggest using a stand mixer or electric beaters.

YOUR FRIDGE

Clear some space in your fridge before starting – enough to take your bowl or banneton. Managing the temperature of your dough allows you to make bread AND have a life! Cold slows down the proving process, which not only gives the flavour and health benefits of long fermentation but also means you can shape/bake your loaf when it suits. Dough that's chilled in the bowl can be scaled and shaped from cold, then proved for a couple of hours. A banneton filled with dough can be baked straight from the fridge.

CONTAINER FOR MEASURING LIQUIDS

This doesn't need to be a measuring jug as liquids (ml) can be weighed as grams (g) – straight into any container.

FLEXIBLE PLASTIC SCRAPER

Essential. A cheap, reusable scraper will bring together flour and water, gather together a sticky dough, tension a dough ball and help to clean up your work surface.

METAL DOUGH SCRAPER

A useful tool for dividing and cutting dough.

FOOD-SAFE PLASTIC BAGS/SHOWER CAP

Use to cover dough while it's proving. If it's going to be in contact with the dough, lightly grease it.

DIGITAL THERMOMETER

Manipulating the temperature of the environment and ingredients enables you to control the rate of fermentation – the key to success.

BAKING PARCHMENT

You can line tins for bread and loaf cakes with a 'sling' of parchment. The short side of your parchment rectangle should be the same as the widest part of your tin, while the length should be the same as the two sides, plus the base, plus 5cm extra on each side for lifting the bread out.

CANE OR WICKER BANNETON

Not an essential, but a nice addition. If you're using a plastic banneton, use a cloth inner.

LINEN TEA TOWEL

Use a well-floured cloth to line a bowl (instead of a banneton) or for proving baguettes/ciabatta.

DUTCH OVEN/HEAVY-BASED CASSEROLE WITH LID

Bake your bread inside one of these and you'll achieve consistently good results. It's the most effective way of creating a moist, steamy environment for your loaf in the early stages.

SILICONE MATS

These reusable mats are great for lining a baking tray quickly and easily. Interestingly, because they have such a slippery surface cookies tend to spread further, so if this is a problem for you, it may be the mat.

CAKE TINS

Try and use the correct size when you make a recipe for the first time – it can make the difference between a flat, biscuit-like cake or a mess in the bottom of your oven. If you don't have the right size tin, you'll need to increase/decrease your recipe and/or adjust your oven temperatures and timings and accept that it's going to look different from the recipe.

ROLLING PINS

For the lamination process you will require a straight rolling pin without a handle or taper, known as a French rolling pin.

BAKING BEANS

You can buy ceramic beans but they're costly and unnecessary. Line the item you're blind baking with cling film or baking parchment and fill with rice or dried pulses. Keep in a tub (once cool) so you can reuse.

PIPING BAGS

I use disposable bags and reuse them as many times as possible, rinsing them out afterwards. As most icing is piped with a round tip, you can just cut the end off the bag. Keep a selection of sizes.

Brunch

We love the way our customers give structure and rhythm to our days – there's David who'll be waiting as the bolts are pulled back for the first of many 'large flat white' (yes, we know it's not really a 'thing' but we aim to please), Tristan for a quick espresso and a sneaky custard tart and Cyril, regular as clockwork, with the crossword and his morning porridge – we've been making it just how he likes it for ten years now!

Later, we welcome our much-loved holiday crowd, many of them now familiar faces, sitting down for baked eggs and French toast. When it's time to set off, there are more decisions: how many sausage rolls, cheese scones and mini cakes are required for the beach-hut picnic?

Our brunch recipes are perfect for family breakfasts, late risers and food on-the-go.

Apple pie oats

Difficulty: ⏲

Serves: 1
(makes compote and crumble for 4)

Prep: 20 mins
Bake: 15 mins

Apple compote
2 medium Bramley
  apples
2 Granny Smith apples
2–3 tbsp water
80g light brown sugar
Juice of 1 lemon
1 tsp ground
  cinnamon

Apple pie crumble
100g spelt or
  wholemeal flour
50g light brown sugar
1 tsp ground cinnamon
1 tsp mixed spice
½ tsp ground cloves
¼ tsp flaky sea salt
50g unsalted butter,
  cubed
50g rolled oats

Porridge
50g rolled oats
100ml full-fat milk
50ml water

Some people like their porridge thick enough to 'stick to your ribs' and stand a spoon up in. I like mine with creamy puddles around the edge of the bowl, so adjust the milk and water to your preference.

Porridge oats make an incredibly nutritious breakfast. High in protein and rich in antioxidants and soluble fibre, they'll make you feel fuller for longer. Look for rolled oats that cook quickly due to their larger surface area.

The spiced crumble is a doddle to make and also perfect for sprinkling on fresh fruit and yoghurt (or just for munching on quietly when no one's looking).

Peel and chop the apples into 1cm dice and place in a heavy-based pan with the water. Cover the pan and simmer over a gentle heat for a couple of minutes until the Bramley apple softens, stirring occasionally to prevent it sticking.

Add the sugar, lemon juice and cinnamon and continue to gently simmer for another few minutes until the Granny Smith apple is soft but still maintaining its shape. Remove from the heat and cool. The compote will keep in the fridge for up to 5 days and freezes well.

To make the crumble, preheat your oven to 190°C/170°C fan/gas 5. Weigh your flour, sugar, spices and salt into a bowl, then weigh the butter and rub into the dry mix with your fingertips until it resembles coarse breadcrumbs, before adding the oats and combining. Place the crumbs onto a shallow metal tray and bake for 10 minutes. Remove from the oven and roughly stir into clumps, then bake for another 5 minutes until golden brown. Cool completely and store in an airtight tub for up to 2 weeks.

For your porridge, place your oats, milk and water in a heavy-based pan and simmer gently until thick. This will take about 3–5 minutes depending on the make of your oats. Add more water if it's getting too thick.

To serve, spoon your porridge into a wide shallow bowl (it'll cool quicker that way) and finish with a dollop of apple and a scattering of crumble.

Orange, hazelnut and chocolate granola

GF

Difficulty: ⎕
Makes: 12–15 servings

Prep: 30 mins
*(the candied orange
peel needs to be
made ahead)*
Bake: 30–45 mins

130g unsalted butter
150g honey
90g golden syrup
250g light brown sugar
1 tbsp orange
   flower water
200g flaked almonds
250g hazelnuts,
   roughly chopped
1 tsp cardamom
   seeds, ground
500g rolled oats
1 x Candied Orange
   Peel (see page 257)
100g dark chocolate,
   chopped into
   1cm chunks

Dark, bitter chocolate is required here – let's not kid ourselves, this is Coco Pops all grown up! Choose a good-quality orange flower water such as the Cortas brand – the cheap stuff often has a strange chemical taste. Serve with plenty of fresh fruit and yoghurt.

Preheat the oven to 180°C/160°C fan/gas 4.

Place the butter, honey, golden syrup and light brown sugar in a heavy-based pan over a low heat, stirring occasionally until melted and combined. Remove from the heat and stir in the orange flower water.

Place the almonds, chopped hazelnuts, ground cardamom and rolled oats into a heatproof bowl, then add the melted butter mix, stirring well to combine.

Arrange the granola mix in a layer on a couple of rimmed baking sheets and bake for 30–45 minutes until crisp and golden brown, stirring the mixture every 10 minutes to break into small clumps.

When the granola is ready, tip the mix into a large bowl and stir to break up any large chunks. Allow to cool, stirring regularly, then add the orange strips and chocolate.

Store in an airtight container or pack into bags and tie with a pretty ribbon. The granola will keep for up to 6 months.

French toast with mascarpone and amaretto cherries

Difficulty: ☐
Serves: 2

Prep: 35 mins

3 eggs
80ml double cream
80ml full-fat milk
½ tsp vanilla extract
2 x 2cm-thick slices of
  Betsy Bread (see
  page 128) or Brioche
  Loaf (see page 207)
30g unsalted butter
2 tbsp sunflower oil
100g mascarpone
Cherry Amaretto Jam
  (see page 236)
Berries, for
  decoration (optional)
2 tbsp icing sugar

As a boarding school child with parents abroad, I often spent weekends at school friends' houses. Debbie taught me how to make 'eggy bread' for breakfast, her parents kindly letting us trash the kitchen as we dipped white sliced bread into milk and egg and fried it in butter before slathering it in golden syrup – heavenly.

We've taken things to the next level with buttery, sweet brioche becoming the perfect sponge for a rich vanilla custard (though any soft white bread will work fine). Leave plenty of time for the bread to soak up the liquid before gently frying to caramelised perfection.

Heat your oven and place a couple of plates inside to warm.

In a bowl, beat the eggs with the cream, milk and vanilla until combined, then pour into a wide shallow dish.

Dip the bread or brioche slices into the egg mix, allowing them to absorb the liquid for a couple of minutes, then melt half the butter and oil in a large frying pan until sizzling. Add one eggy bread/brioche slice, frying on both sides until golden brown. Remove from the pan when fully cooked, keeping it warm in the oven while you melt the remaining butter/oil and fry the remaining soaked slice.

Serve the toast with a scoop of mascarpone and the jam. Serve with berries, if desired, and dredge the whole plate with icing sugar.

GF

Spicy East Coast egg and beans

Difficulty: ▢
Serves: 4

Prep: 45 mins
*(the sauce can
be made ahead)*
Bake: 10–15 mins

4 eggs
2 ripe avocados
100g crème fraîche
1 lime, halved
2 fresh red or green
chillies, sliced

Spicy beans
3 tbsp sunflower oil
1 small red onion,
cut into small dice
1 red or green pepper,
deseeded and cut
into 5mm slices
1 garlic clove, finely
chopped
1 tbsp ground
sweet paprika
1 tsp ground cumin
¼ tsp chilli flakes
2 tbsp tomato purée
400g tin chopped
tomatoes
1 tsp red wine vinegar
1 tbsp light brown sugar
400g tin cannellini or
pinto beans, drained
and rinsed
½ tsp flaky sea salt
¼ tsp black pepper
Large handful of fresh
coriander

**Bold flavours make the perfect start to the weekend – full of colour, heat
and sparkle. Add extra eggs for hungry people. Serve with slices of
buttered sourdough toast and bask in the praise as everyone dives in.
Make the sauce ahead and freeze or store in the fridge for up to 3 days.
Reheat until bubbling, then add your eggs before finishing in the oven.**

To make the spicy beans, heat the oil in a medium-sized heavy-based pan.
Add the chopped onion, sliced pepper and garlic. Gently fry for about
5 minutes until softened but not browned, then add the spices and cook for
another couple of minutes. Add the rest of the ingredients, except for the
fresh coriander, and simmer on a low heat for 30–40 minutes until the sauce
is reduced and quite dry. Set aside some coriander leaves for serving, then
roughly chop the rest of the coriander leaves and stalks and add to the beans
with seasoning to taste. Cool and refrigerate until required.

When you're ready to eat, preheat the oven to 240°C/220°C fan/gas 9.

This is a dish for everyone to share, so warm your beans in a wide, shallow
ovenproof dish or a 20–25cm shallow ovenproof pan. Once the beans are
bubbling, push some of the sauce to one side with a spoon to create four
craters and crack an egg (or two) into each one. Place the pan, uncovered,
into the hot oven for 10–15 minutes. Remove from the oven when the egg
whites are set but the yolks are still runny.

While the eggs are baking, peel the avocados, halve and remove the stones.
Slice each half thinly from end to end. Place a generous dollop of crème
fraîche alongside each egg, arrange the avocado on top, then follow with
a good squeeze of lime juice. Chop the remaining coriander leaves and
sprinkle over with the chilli and more flaky sea salt and black pepper.

Mushrooms and Binham Blue tartine

Difficulty: ⏾
Serves: 2

....

Prep: 20 mins

....

1 tbsp olive oil
100g chestnut
  mushrooms, cut into
  1cm slices
1 large banana shallot,
  finely sliced
1 garlic clove, finely
  sliced
1 tsp fresh thyme,
  stalks removed
100ml double cream
100g Binham Blue
  cheese, crumbled
2 thick slices of Classic
  Magpie Sourdough
  (see page 137)
100g watercress
5–6 pickled silverskin
  onions, halved, per
  person
Flaky sea salt

We love a tartine – it's essentially stuff on toast and makes the perfect showcase for our bread and an opportunity to let simple seasonal ingredients speak for themselves. Mrs Temple's Binham Blue is a creamy Norfolk cow's milk cheese that crumbles softly. If you can't find it, then Cambozola or Dolcelatte would be great substitutes. Thanks to Ali, our Southwold chef, for this recipe – our customers love you for it!

Heat the oil in a heavy-based pan, then add the sliced mushrooms, shallot, garlic, thyme and a generous grind of flaky sea salt and black pepper. Cook gently for 5 minutes until the shallot has softened.

Add the cream and crumbled cheese and continue to cook gently for another 5 minutes.

Toast the sourdough bread and lay each slice on a warmed plate. Top with the cooked mushroom mix. Season generously with salt and black pepper.

Garnish with a handful of peppery watercress and sharp pickled onions.

Boozy buck rarebit

Difficulty: ⬠

Serves: 2

....

Prep: 20 mins

....

50g unsalted butter

100g plain flour

250ml Ghost Ship pale
ale, warmed

250g mature Cheddar
cheese, grated

½ tsp Dijon mustard

½ tsp ground
cayenne pepper

1 tsp Worcestershire
sauce

1 tsp white wine vinegar

2 eggs, as fresh
as possible

2 slices of Classic
Magpie Sourdough
(see page 137)

Salad leaves

1 tbsp olive oil

Squeeze of lemon juice

Flaky sea salt

Adnams brewery, just around the corner from our Southwold bakery, is cleverly disguised behind a row of Victorian house facades. Walking past, dodging the brewery guides steering their charges, the malty smell of the mash and the whooshing clanking noises of the brewery filter through those long-closed front doors, permeating the salty sea air.

My bakery friend Karen taught me this method for poaching eggs the morning after an evening of cocktails in her newly converted post-lockdown 'bar' (AKA garden shed). I'd like to say the evening was memorable, but that would be missing the point. What was memorable was the method for softly poached eggs served with hot, buttery toast and a large mug of tea. The perfect antidote.

The brief boiling period stops the whites going stringy in the water and if your eggs are fresh, you'll have perfect results every time.

Melt the butter and flour in a small, heavy-based pan and stir to create a slurry. Cook over a gentle heat for a few minutes, then gradually add the warm pale ale, stirring rapidly with each addition. When all the liquid is incorporated, add the cheese, Dijon, cayenne and Worcestershire sauce. Continue to stir as the sauce bubbles and thickens. Season to taste with salt and plenty of black pepper. Allow the sauce to cool completely.

When you're ready to eat, preheat the grill to medium hot. Place a small pan of water on the hob for your poached eggs and add the white wine vinegar. When you start to see bubbles rising from the bottom of the pan, place your whole (unshelled) eggs in carefully, using a spoon. Turn the heat right down until the surface of the water is very gently simmering and count to 10. Using a spoon, remove the eggs from the pan and stir the water to create a whirlpool. Now break your eggs into the whirlpool, one after the other, and very gently simmer for 3–4 minutes, depending on how soft you like your yolk. Carefully remove each egg using a slotted spoon and place on some kitchen paper to drain.

While your eggs are cooking, toast your bread until lightly golden, then spread a generous dollop of cheese sauce on the top of each slice – about 2cm thick. Place under the hot grill until bubbling and golden brown, then place your perfect poached eggs on top.

Dress the salad leaves with the oil, a pinch of flaky sea salt and black pepper and a squeeze of lemon juice. Serve with the rarebit to cut through the rich cheesiness.

Pink grapefruit, frisée, pecans and Gorgonzola

Difficulty: ⬚
Serves: 2

....

Prep: 20 mins

....

80g pecan nuts, halved
2 tbsp maple syrup
1 pink grapefruit
2 tbsp olive oil
½ tsp flaky sea salt
¼ tsp black pepper
2 thick slices of Classic
  Magpie Sourdough
  (see page 137)
40g salted butter
Radicchio
Frisée (curly endive)
  lettuce
150g Gorgonzola
  cheese, cubed
Flaky sea salt

Such a pretty plate. Slivers of the palest pink peep out from a red and green froth of bitter leaves. Nuggets of candied pecans add sweetness and crunch. Make sure you bring the ripe Gorgonzola to room temperature – you're after oozy dollops.

Preheat the oven to 190°C/170°C fan/gas 5.

Place the pecan halves on a rimmed baking sheet and combine with the maple syrup and a pinch of flaky sea salt. Bake for 5 minutes until the sugar has caramelised slightly. Watch closely, they burn quickly!

Supreme the grapefruit by trimming the top and bottom, then slicing lengthways between the flesh and the peel, following the curve of the fruit and removing all peel and pith. Hold the grapefruit over a bowl and use a small sharp knife to slice lengthways towards the centre of the fruit, cutting between each segment and its membrane. Repeat on the other side of each segment so that you can remove it in one piece with the knife blade. Repeat around the whole fruit, then squeeze the juice from the empty membrane (approximately 2 tablespoons) and combine with the olive oil, salt and black pepper and whisk lightly.

Toast the bread, spread thickly with butter and top with the radicchio and frisée. Garnish with the grapefruit segments, candied pecans and Gorgonzola, then finish with the grapefruit dressing.

Baron Bigod with pears, walnuts and truffle honey

Difficulty: ⌂
Serves: 2

Prep: 20 mins

50 walnut halves
1 ripe Conference pear
2 thick slices of Classic
 Magpie Sourdough
 (see page 137)
Salted butter, for
 spreading
200g Baron Bigod brie
 cheese
Salad leaves
1 tbsp olive oil
Squeeze of lemon juice
1 tbsp truffle honey
Balsamic Fig Chutney
 (see page 244)
Flaky sea salt

If you've never tried truffle honey, take it from me, it's worth tracking down. I'm stating the obvious when I say it's sweet, but it's also earthy with an intoxicating aroma. Stick a spoon in the jar and serve it with a cheese board, drizzle over a cheesy pizza (see page 168, the Annie) or over this tartine.

Baron Bigod brie is a delicious soft raw cheese, made by Jonny and Dulcie Crickmore in Bungay just down the road from us. We're so pleased Fen Farm Dairy has become a recognised name on the (cheese) map in recent years – we're big fans of their buttermilk, too. If you can't find Baron Bigod, then any ripe, tasty brie will make a good substitute.

Preheat the oven to 190°C/170°C fan/gas 5.

Place the walnut halves on a rimmed baking sheet and toast until fragrant – 5–8 minutes. Keep a close eye on them – they burn easily.

Wash the pear, then core and slice into eight, leaving the skin on. If preparing ahead, then place the cut pear in cold water with a squeeze of lemon juice.

Preheat the grill to medium hot. Toast the bread and spread with butter. Slice the Brie thickly to cover the toast and place under the grill until the cheese is bubbling. Dress the salad leaves with the oil, a pinch of flaky sea salt and black pepper and a squeeze of lemon juice.

Place the toast on plates, top with the pear and walnuts and drizzle the truffle honey over the melting cheese. Serve with the salad leaves, chutney and a good grind of black pepper.

Smørrebrød

The seaside town of Skagen is a delight – low yellow houses with red roof tiles and white picket fences nestle deep in the dunes. Situated on the Jutland peninsula at the tip of Denmark, it's traditional to risk life and limb by standing at the point where two seas meet (the charmingly named Skagerrak and Kattegat). It's also traditional to eat open sandwiches (Smørrebrød) and in the small café on the main street, they were the only choice. The 'menu' was a cheap tear-off note pad. Pencils were provided and the pad was divided vertically – toppings on the left side with a box to tick on the right – a bit like choosing from the Argos catalogue. The list was extensive and the sandwiches that arrived were magnificent, with toppings ranging from the ordinary (eggs, smoked salmon and potatoes) to the extraordinary (grilled eel, smoked tongue and brains).

Smørrebrød literally translates as 'buttered bread'. The butter gives important flavour and texture, so make sure it's delicious and spread it thickly right to the edges of the bread.

Use a dense, flavoursome rye bread for these sandwiches, such as the Torte de Seigle on page 144. How many slices required per person will depend on your appetite and the shape of your loaf!

Beetroot, feta and blackberry smørrebrød

Difficulty: ◯
Serves: 2

Prep: 20 mins
Infusing: 2 hrs
Bake: 1 hr

50g hazelnuts
Zest of 1 orange
250ml olive oil
1 tsp honey
1 tsp balsamic vinegar
150g cooked beetroot
30g salted butter
2 thin slices of Torte de
   Seigle sourdough
   (see page 144)
50g rocket leaves
100g feta cheese
75g blackberries
4 radishes, thinly sliced
Fresh herbs, chopped
   (optional)
Flaky sea salt

This little beauty showcases the autumnal flavours and colours of beetroot, blackberries and hazelnuts with salty crumbled feta cheese and a sweet orange and honey dressing. If time allows, I'd recommend you cook the roots yourself rather than buy a vac pack. Wash them, remove the stems (great for using later) and roast, skin on, until tender, then peel when cool. They're also delicious roughly chopped and served warm, dressed with tasty olive oil, fresh herbs and plenty of seasoning.

Preheat the oven to 190°C/170°C fan/gas 5.

Place the hazelnuts in a shallow tray and roast until toasted and fragrant – check them after 5 minutes so they don't get too dark or they'll become bitter. Allow to cool, then chop roughly.

Zest your orange and stir into the olive oil with a pinch of flaky sea salt, black pepper, the honey and balsamic vinegar. Do this a couple of hours ahead of time to give the flavours time to mingle.

If you're using a bunch of fresh beetroot, roast until tender for an hour or so, then remove the skins. Once your beetroot is cool (or use a pack of boiled beetroot) slice into 2mm discs.

Liberally butter your rye bread right to the edges. Arrange most of your rocket leaves on the bread, then lay your beetroot slices on top, overlapping them to give height.

Crumble the feta in chunks over the beetroot slices, then tuck some blackberries between the layers. Give the orange dressing a quick whisk, then drizzle over the top.

Dress the plate with a couple more rocket leaves, the radishes and fresh herbs, if using.

Egg and anchovy smørrebrød

Difficulty: ◻
Serves: 2

Prep: 30 mins

250g small waxy
potatoes
100g sour cream
Small bunch of fresh
dill, finely chopped
Small bunch of fresh
chives, finely chopped
2 large eggs
60g salted butter
2 thin slices of Torte de
Seigle sourdough
(see page 144)
50g watercress
8 whole salted
anchovies
1 tbsp capers in
brine, drained, plus
extra to garnish
½ small red onion, very
thinly sliced
6 radishes, thinly sliced
Flaky sea salt

There's a wonderfully old-fashioned anchovy paste that goes by the name of 'Patum Peperium' – AKA Gentleman's Relish. The packaging for this pungent paste is delightfully archaic and the name clearly a throwback to a previous un-woke era! Even if you're a stalwart of the anchovy fan club (which I clearly am), just the tip of a knife is all that's required, spread on hot buttered toast, cut into soldiers and dipped in a softly boiled egg.

Egg and anchovies clearly have a fan base the world over – this sandwich brings those flavours to life Scandinavian-style.

Place a pan of salted water on the hob to boil while you scrub the potatoes, leaving the skins on. Make sure they're a similar size so they cook evenly. When the water is boiling, add to the pan and cook for 15–20 minutes until tender when pierced with a sharp knife. Cool the potatoes under running cold water, then drain.

Mix the sour cream with most of the chopped herbs, leaving some for the garnish, and season to taste with flaky sea salt and black pepper.

Place a pan of water on the hob and add your eggs when it comes to the boil. Cook the eggs for 6 minutes, then run under cold water until cool.

Liberally butter your rye bread right to the edges.

Thickly spread the sour cream over the bread, then arrange your watercress on top. Slice the cooled potatoes and lay overlapping discs onto the watercress to give height to your creation.

Peel the eggs, slice thinly and arrange on top of the potatoes. Tear the anchovies in half and arrange on top of the egg.

Tuck the capers into the nooks and crannies and add the remaining dill and chives to garnish. Finish with a good pinch of flaky sea salt and a generous grind of black pepper. Garnish the plate with the onion, extra capers and the radishes.

Smoked salmon, pickled onion and samphire smørrebrød

Difficulty: ⏻
Serves: 2

Prep: 30 mins

1 small red onion
100ml white wine or
 cider vinegar
1 tbsp caster sugar
1 tsp fine table salt
60g salted butter
2 thin slices of Torte de
 Seigle sourdough
 (see page 144)
70g cream cheese
120g smoked salmon
15g samphire
2 tbsp capers in brine,
 drained, plus extra
 to garnish
Several generous fronds
 of fresh dill
½ lemon, cut into
 wedges
Flaky sea salt

Mustard dressing
2 tbsp Dijon mustard
1 tbsp honey
2 tbsp olive oil
1 tsp lemon juice
½ tsp flaky sea salt
Few grinds of black
 pepper

Use the best-quality salmon you can get your hands on and you really can't go wrong with this classic combo. Take time to arrange and build up the colourful layers to create height and texture – you're making an edible work of art.

Slice the onion in half downwards from the top, then peel the skin away, leaving the root attached. Lay the cut side down and slice very thinly into semi-circles. Weigh the vinegar into a non-reactive bowl, add the sugar and salt and stir to dissolve. Place the sliced onion in the bowl and leave for at least 20 minutes and up to a couple of days (if refrigerated).

Mix all the mustard dressing ingredients together.

Liberally butter your rye bread right to the edges. Thickly spread the cream cheese over the bread, then arrange your smoked salmon on top – create vertical waves with the salmon to give height to the sandwich.

Arrange most of your drained pickled onions, samphire and capers on top. Finish with a generous splash of mustard dressing, fresh dill fronds, black pepper and a pinch of flaky sea salt.

Garnish the plate with a couple more capers, semi-circles of pickled red onion and a wedge of lemon.

Winter panzanella

Difficulty: ⏻
Serves: 4

. . . .

Prep: 1 hr

. . . .

1 large butternut squash
2 small/medium red
   onions
3 tbsp olive oil
250g speckled brown
   or puy lentils
1 garlic clove, sliced
3 bay leaves
150ml extra virgin
   olive oil
2 tbsp balsamic vinegar
1 tbsp Dijon mustard
½ tsp flaky sea salt
¼ tsp black pepper
500g any sourdough
   bread
200g green beans
250g feta cheese,
   crumbled
Large bunch of fresh
   flat-leaf parsley,
   chopped
Pinch of chilli flakes
1 fresh red chilli,
   thinly sliced
Zest of 1 lemon
100g sunflower seeds,
   toasted

Our students produce mountains of bread during our sourdough bread class. We always serve them a seasonal version of this fortifying salad for lunch to show them a delicious way to use up leftovers. Serve slightly warm or at room temperature with a leafy salad.

Preheat the oven to 210°C/190°C fan/gas 6–7.

Halve the butternut squash and remove the seeds. Cut side down, slice into 2cm-thick sections, then into 2cm cubes and place in a large roasting tray. Peel and cut the red onions into wedges with the root still attached and add to the roasting tray. Add the olive oil and a sprinkle of sea salt and black pepper and toss the vegetables to coat well. Roast for 30–40 minutes until tender and slightly charred. Allow to cool.

Meanwhile, rinse the lentils thoroughly in a sieve, removing any grit. Place in a pan with 500ml of water, the garlic and bay leaves. Bring to the boil, then simmer gently, removing any scum, for 25–30 minutes until the lentils are tender but still with a little bite. Drain and run under cold water to cool.

Mix the extra virgin olive oil, balsamic vinegar, Dijon mustard, sea salt and black pepper. Pour half of the dressing over the warm lentils and stir gently.

Remove the crusts from the bread and slice into chunky 3cm cubes. Place in the cooling heat of the oven to crisp and dry out or prepare the day before and cover with a tea towel.

Boil a small pan of water with a generous pinch of salt. Blanch the green beans until slightly tender (no squeak!) but still bright green. Drain under running cold water until cool.

Combine the dressed lentils with half the roast butternut squash, half the beans, half the feta, most of the parsley (reserve a little for garnish) and all the bread, roast onion and chilli flakes.

Place in a large serving bowl and dot with the remaining squash, feta and beans. Pour over the remaining dressing, check the seasoning and garnish with the remaining parsley, the sliced chilli, grated lemon zest and a sprinkling of toasted sunflower seeds.

Spicy spinach empanadas

These were inspired by saag aloo, the spinach and potato stalwart of Indian restaurants everywhere. The distinctive flavour comes from the spice mix, known as panch phoran in east India and Bangladesh.

Difficulty: ⬭⬭⬭
Makes: 10

Prep: 2 hrs
Chill: 2 hrs or overnight
+ 30 mins
Bake: 20–25 mins

100g white onions, thinly
  sliced in semi-circles
1 tbsp sunflower oil
200g spinach
600g new (waxy)
  potatoes
400g tin chickpeas,
  drained and rinsed
1 tsp ground ginger
1 tsp mixed spice
¼ tsp ground turmeric
1 tsp flaky sea salt
¼ tsp black pepper
Egg Wash (see
  page 251)
100g nigella seeds

Pastry
170g plain flour
120g unsalted butter,
  cut into 1cm cubes
½ tsp fine table salt
½ tsp caster sugar
20g egg yolk (1 egg)
120ml double cream

Panch phoran spice mix
1 tsp each mustard,
  fennel, fenugreek,
  nigella and cumin
  seeds

To make the pastry, combine the flour, butter, salt and sugar using the paddle on a stand mixer or by rubbing between your fingertips until the butter pieces are the size of a pea – it's OK to see pieces of fat in the dough. Combine the yolk and cream and add to the flour, mix briefly and stop as soon as the dough comes together. Do not overmix or it will be tough. Press into a block 3cm high. Wrap in paper or plastic and chill for a few hours or overnight.

Combine the onion with the oil and a pinch of salt and black pepper in a small pan. Cook gently for 15 minutes until soft but not browned. Remove any woody stalks from the spinach, then wash. Place in a heatproof bowl, cover and microwave for 1 minute or steam until wilted (1–2 minutes). Leave covered until cool, then drain and squeeze out all excess water.

Place the potatoes, unpeeled, in a pan of salted water and bring to the boil. Simmer for 15–20 minutes until tender. Drain and leave to cool. When cool enough to handle, use a potato masher or metal dough cutter to crush slightly.

Place the panch phoran seeds in a frying pan and toast until fragrant and popping. Remove from the heat. In a bowl, combine the chickpeas, toasted spices, spinach, onion, potato, ground spices and seasoning.

Roll out the rested and chilled pastry to a 60cm square and cut out nine discs, each 18cm in diameter and 3mm thick (use a side plate or bowl to cut around). Re-roll the remaining pastry and cut out the remaining disc. Place a 100g portion of the potato mix in the centre of each pastry disc. Using a pastry brush, spread the egg wash around the edges of each disc, then fold it in half to enclose the filling. Crimp the edge of the semi-circle using your fingers and thumbs. Chill for at least 30 minutes before baking or freeze and bake straight from frozen.

Preheat the oven to 195°C/175°C fan/gas 5–6.

Brush the empanadas with egg wash, then dip the crimped edges in nigella seeds to create a delicate rim, like the lace on a pair of lady's knickers. Place on a baking tray, slightly spaced. Bake for 20–25 minutes until golden.

Pork and apricot sausage rolls

Difficulty: ⬜⬜⬜
Makes: 10
(pastry made the day before)

Prep: 30 mins
Chill: 2 hrs
Bake: 35–40 mins

1kg Puff Pastry
  (see page 250)
Egg Wash (see
  page 251)

Filling
600g pork sausage
  meat
80g sourdough
  breadcrumbs
200g white onions,
  chopped into
  5mm cubes
80g dried apricots,
  chopped into
  3mm cubes
20g caster sugar
1 tbsp herbes
  de Provence
1 garlic clove, finely
  chopped
1 tsp sea salt
½ tsp black pepper

Bakeries aren't for the faint-hearted. As if hefting heavy sacks of flour and hauling dough out of the mixer wasn't enough, in the early days we used a piping bag to portion the mix for our sausage rolls. This was manageable when making 30 or 40 at a time, but as their popularity grew, we developed biceps Popeye would have been proud of. Eventually we found the answer to our prayers: a beautiful red-and-chrome hand-cranked sausage-making machine that never tires.

Make the puff pastry the day before and allow to chill overnight if possible.

Combine all the filling ingredients and leave to rest in the fridge for a couple of hours to soften the breadcrumbs and bind the mixture.

Roll out the pastry to a 50cm x 32cm rectangle with the long side next to your body. Make a small notch on both short sides 8cm up from the bottom edge and then 8cm down from the top edge. This gives you a guideline for where to lay your sausage meat. Place a bowl of water close by and wet your hands each time you handle the sausage meat. Divide it into two sausage-shaped portions and place each one level with the notched sides. You will now have two lines of filling laid out on your puff pastry.

Using a pastry brush and water, brush a horizontal line across the centre of the puff pastry about 3cm wide. Lift the lower long edge of pastry, folding it over the sausage meat to enclose it, pressing the long edge down all along the central line. Repeat this action on the top half of the dough, lifting the long edge over the sausage and pressing it along the central line. Both logs of sausage will now be enclosed in puff pastry and joined in the centre.

Run a knife horizontally down the centre to divide the two meat logs, then cut five sausage rolls from each log. Score the top of each roll with some quick knife slashes, then store in the fridge (or freezer) until ready to bake.

Preheat the oven to 210°C/190°C fan/gas 6–7.

Place the rolls on a baking sheet with space in between. Add a pinch of salt to the egg wash and brush over. Bake for 25 minutes, then turn the tray and bake for another 10–15 minutes until crisp and golden brown. Check the internal temperature is 75°C or more before removing from the oven.

Cheese and chive scones

Difficulty: ⬭
Makes: 8

Prep: 30 mins
Bake: 25–30 mins

Equipment: 10cm cutter

500g plain flour
1 tbsp baking powder
35g caster sugar
1 tsp caraway seeds
1 tsp smoked paprika
½ tsp fine table salt
100g cold unsalted
  butter, cut into
  1cm cubes
250g mature Cheddar
  cheese, coarsely
  grated
4 tbsp snipped
  fresh chives
1 egg
240ml full-fat milk,
  plus 2 tbsp

Our cheese scones have a secret ingredient but we don't keep the recipe under lock and key or swear our pastry team to secrecy – it's even written on the label for everyone to see. This ingredient has a distinctive flavour that makes cheese taste even cheesier, but if they were called 'Cheese, chive and caraway scones' would you buy them? Thought not. You can keep it a secret, too.

In a large bowl (or your stand mixer with the paddle attachment), weigh the flour, baking powder, sugar, caraway seeds, paprika and salt. Add the butter and rub in very briefly – stop while you can still see pea-sized pieces of butter.

Add 200g of the cheese (reserve the rest) and the chives and mix briefly to combine, then whisk the egg and milk together and pour in. Mix very briefly until the dough starts to come together but some dry bits remain.

Turn the dough out onto the counter and press it with your fingers to a flattish shape about 4cm thick, pushing any dry bits into the mix. Fold the dough in half over itself, then press out again. Repeat the fold and press another two times, finishing with the dough at a height of 4cm.

Place a small bowl with extra plain flour close by. Dip a 10cm plain cutter into the flour each time you cut out a scone. Cut straight down onto the counter – don't twist the dough. You can freeze the scones at this stage. Let them sit at room temperature for half an hour when baking from frozen.

Preheat your oven to 195°C/175°C fan/gas 5–6.

Place the scones onto a greased baking tray, leaving a 3cm space between them. By placing them close together, they support each other and don't spread so much as they bake. Brush the tops with the extra milk and sprinkle over the remaining grated cheese.

Bake for 25–30 minutes, turning the tray after 20 minutes, until golden brown. A skewer inserted in the middle should come out clean.

The
Sweet
Spot

Nobody needs cake but a love for sweetness is written into our DNA and a bountiful shop window is hard to resist. It's fascinating watching someone go through the selection process – there's no doubt that we eat with our eyes. From the initial germ of an idea to the final decision, this pleasurable non-essential act certainly makes us opinionated.

First, there's the abrupt stop as they're strolling past the window, then a quick discussion with willing accomplices – fingers pointing, faces pressed against the window.

The next step is entering the shop and realising that there's even more choices inside – more indecision – not helped by partners who are frantically tapping on the window to get attention. What started out as just an impulse has quickly become serious as the pros and cons of each option are weighed up. Then, finally, the choice(s) – helped by comments from our front-of-house team – after all, treats are always zero calories when you're on holiday, right?!

Whether you're buying, making or receiving a cake, it's always an act of kindness, generosity and pleasure.

We're regularly asked if we can share our recipes as many customers are visitors to Suffolk and don't have the option of popping in to pick up their favourite treat. When I can, I do, though many recipes are a little more involved and technical than a quick scribble on the back of an envelope. This chapter contains the know-how for many of our most popular cookies, cakes, bars and tarts, so if you're wanting a little reminder of your holiday or just need a little extra sweetness in your life, you're in the right place.

Brown butter nutmeg shortbread

Difficulty: ⬜⬜
Makes: 20

Prep: 30 mins
Chill: 30 mins–24 hrs
Bake: 25–30 mins

230g unsalted butter
80g light brown sugar
80g caster sugar
½ tsp fine sea salt
250g plain flour
80g fine semolina
2 tsp grated nutmeg,
 plus extra
50g demerara sugar

Nutmeg, with its intense, spicy flavour, is often reserved for the bread sauce at Christmas. If yours lives in a dusty spice jar at the back of your cupboard, treat yourself to a whole nutmeg. Simply rub the nut over the fine side of a grater and enjoy the nose-tickling aroma.
 These caramelised, buttery, crumbly squares will have you licking your fingers and chasing sugary crumbs around your plate.

Brown butter – what is it and why?

Bringing butter to a frothing, foaming boil for a couple of minutes caramelises the milk solids and adds a nutty, butterscotch flavour to your baking. Consider doing this whenever a recipe calls for melted butter – just remember that the boiling process causes water in the butter to evaporate, so you may need to balance this reduction with other ingredients.

Have a heavy-duty plastic or ceramic heatproof mixing bowl at the ready for your butter to be tipped into – lightweight plastic bowls melt! The bowl will cool the butter down quickly once it's the perfect caramel colour – a minute or two longer in the pan can cause it to blacken and become bitter.

Place the butter in a medium-sized pan and bring to the boil. Allow it to bubble fiercely for 5–8 minutes, scraping the bottom with a spatula regularly. When it starts to smell sweet and nutty and the boiling foam rises up in the pan, pour the hot liquid (including the brown flecks and scrapings from the bottom) into the bowl. Cool, stirring occasionally as it firms up.

Weigh the sugars and the salt into a bowl, add the cooled butter and gently beat until smooth. Add the flour, semolina and nutmeg and beat briefly only until the mix comes together and clears the sides of the bowl. Do not overmix. Tip into a greased and lined 23cm x 23cm x 5cm square baking tin and press gently with your fingertips to cover the base of the tin evenly. Use a fork to prick the shortbread all over, then chill for 30 minutes or up to 1 day.

Preheat the oven to 200°C/180°C fan/gas 6.

Grate nutmeg over the surface, then sprinkle with the demerara sugar. Bake in the centre of the oven for 25–30 minutes, turning the tin after 15 minutes, until pale golden. Cool in the tin before cutting into 20 pieces. These will keep in an airtight tin for up to 3 days or freeze in a covered container on the day of baking and store for 6 months.

Chocolate malt and rye cookies

Difficulty: ⬚
Makes: 12

Prep: 30 mins
Chill: 24–48 hrs
Bake: 12–14 mins

Rye crumbs
200g Rye Bread (such as Torte de Seigle), crusts removed (see page 144)
30g light brown sugar
2 tsp malt powder (Horlicks or similar)
30g melted unsalted butter

Cookie dough
140g caster sugar
20g malt extract
2 eggs
1 egg yolk
140g plain flour
140g strong white bread flour
½ tsp bicarbonate of soda
½ tsp fine sea salt
250g soft unsalted butter, cubed
140g light brown sugar
200g dark chocolate chips
10g flaky sea salt

There's a traditional Danish breakfast dish called ymerdrys. The 'ymer' refers to yoghurt on which the 'drys' (toasted and sweetened rye breadcrumbs) are sprinkled. I'm always looking for new ways to use bread, so the next time I had a stale rye loaf I made these caramelised rye crumbs. The smell of the crumbs toasting was irresistible – it was impossible to keep the experiment under wraps. You know you're onto something when even the most sceptical members of the team keep coming back for more. The consensus was unanimous – we had to come up with a recipe to incorporate them.

While ymerdrys are wonderful added to your breakfast fruit and yoghurt, I can report that they're also delicious added to brownie batter, scattered on ice cream or munched straight from the tin.

Preheat the oven to 210°C/190°C fan/gas 6–7.

Prepare your crumbs by chopping the bread into small cubes. Place in the bowl of a food processor with the sugar and malt powder and pulse to breadcrumbs. Place on a rimmed baking sheet and toast for 10 minutes, tossing the contents after 5 minutes.

Remove the tray and drizzle over the butter, tossing the crumbs to coat. Continue to toast for a few more minutes until a deep golden brown. They can burn very quickly towards the end, so stand by the oven! Cool.

In the bowl of your stand mixer, beat the caster sugar, malt extract, eggs and yolk until the ribbon stage. Meanwhile, weigh the plain and bread flours, bicarbonate of soda and salt into a bowl and whisk to combine. When the egg mix is thick, switch to the beater attachment, add the butter and brown sugar and beat to combine. The mix may look like it's split, but go ahead now and fold in the flour mix with a spatula, followed by the chocolate and rye crumbs. Take care not to overmix, keeping your folding to the bare minimum. Chill for at least 24 hours, but 48 is even better.

Preheat the oven to 190°C/170°C fan/gas 5.

Place two baking trays in the oven. Scoop approx. 100g cookies (12 in total) and space them apart on the hot trays. Sprinkle over sea salt and bake for 12–14 minutes, turning the trays after 10 minutes. Cool on the trays. These will keep in an airtight tin for up to 3 days or freeze in a covered container on the day of baking and store for 6 months.

Spiced double chocolate cookies

Difficulty: ⏻
Makes: 14

Prep: 30 mins
Chill: 24–48 hrs
Bake: 12–14 mins

290g soft unsalted
butter
260g caster sugar
260g light brown sugar
190g strong white
bread flour
190g plain flour
140g cocoa powder
½ tsp ground cinnamon
¼ tsp each grated
nutmeg, ground
cardamom and
ground white pepper
1 tsp bicarbonate
of soda
1 tsp baking powder
½ tsp fine sea salt
40g full-fat milk
250g dark chocolate,
roughly chopped
½ tsp flaky sea salt

I love to watch the recipients of these cookies rifling through their flavour memory bank, seeking to put a name to the layered spice flavours in their mouth. These'll keep tickling your taste buds and have you coming back for more. Inspired by lebkuchen, a festive German cookie, you don't have to wait till Christmas to enjoy them.

These cookies work well with a vegan butter block, plant-based milk and dairy-free chocolate substitutions and use some strong bread flour to create a slightly chewier cookie – just the way we like it. The cookie dough keeps well in the fridge for a week, or you can freeze the dough balls and defrost slightly to soften before baking.

Place the butter and two sugars in a bowl or your stand mixer. Gently beat until the mix is well creamed but not airy (otherwise the cookies may collapse when baked).

Weigh and sift the two flours, cocoa powder, all the spices, the bicarbonate of soda, baking powder and salt, then whisk together to combine. Add the dry mix to the butter mix in three additions, alternating with the milk between each addition. Beat briefly to combine the ingredients but don't overmix. Add 200g of the roughly chopped dark chocolate (reserving the rest for later) and briefly mix to combine. Place in your fridge to mature for at least 24 hours but 48 is even better.

Preheat your oven to 190°C/170°C fan/gas 5.

Place two baking sheets in the oven. Scoop the cookies to approx. 100g each (14 in total) and briefly roll each one into a ball between your hands. Remove the sheets from the oven and carefully place the cookies onto the hot sheets, smooshing them down slightly as you push a few chunks of the remaining chocolate into the top of each one. Add a pinch of flaky sea salt and bake for 12–14 minutes, turning the sheets after 10 minutes. Cool on the sheets.

Uncooked, these cookies will keep for up to a week in your fridge and freeze well once they've been shaped. You can also bake them directly from frozen, just add a couple of minutes to the bake time.

Ginger folk

Difficulty: ⭕
Makes: 12

....

Prep: 30 mins
Chill: 2 hrs
Bake: 10–12 mins

....

Equipment: Cutters
   Piping bag

....

130g light brown sugar
50g golden syrup
25g treacle
25ml boiling water
1 tsp ground cinnamon
1 tsp ground ginger
⅛ tsp ground cloves
1 tsp orange zest
150g soft unsalted butter
1 tsp bicarbonate
   of soda, sifted
290g plain flour, sifted
100g icing sugar
3 tsp lemon juice
Red, green and pink
   writing icing
Melted chocolate,
   for icing

Our gingerbread dough morphs between cubist pre-Raphaelite beauties, bony Halloween ghouls and a festive 'Chrismoose'. We also use the dough to construct magical gingerbread houses and the offcuts are great for spicy rocky road and for crumbling over cakes and custards.

Thanks to Richard and Kate of Holtwhites Bakery for the original version of this recipe. Curious visiting bakers who've become firm bakery friends.

Place the sugar, syrup, treacle, hot water, spices and zest in a medium-sized heavy-based pan. Bring to the boil, stirring regularly to prevent the sugar from burning.

Remove the pan from the heat and gradually stir in the soft butter until completely melted. Add the sifted bicarbonate of soda, beating the mix briefly. Add the plain flour in three additions until fully combined. Turn the mix onto the counter and knead briefly until smooth and shiny.

Mould the dough into a rectangle 2cm high, wrap in cling film or baking parchment and place in the fridge for a couple of hours until cold and firm.

Preheat your oven to 180°C/160°C fan/gas 4.

Remove the dough from the fridge and roll out to 3mm thick. Cut out your shapes and lay them on a lined baking sheet, spaced slightly apart.

Bake for 10–12 minutes, turning the tray after 8 minutes. The gingerbread should be a light golden brown and move slightly if you push the edge of a shape. Remove from the oven and cool on the tray.

Combine the icing sugar and lemon juice and mix to create a stiff water icing for decorating. Use a piping bag or a piece of baking parchment to make a small piping bag and pipe lines of icing onto the biscuits, then decorate with writing icing and piped melted chocolate. Leave to set. These will keep in an airtight tin for up to 3 days or freeze in a covered container on the day of baking and store for 6 months.

Raspberry rose lovehearts

Difficulty: ⬭
Makes: 14

Prep: 30 mins
Bake: 8–10 mins

Equipment: Cutters
  Piping bag

340g soft unsalted
  butter
270g caster sugar
½ tsp fine table salt
1 tsp vanilla extract
2 eggs
670g plain flour, sifted
200g Raspberry Vanilla
  Jam (see page 239)
1 tbsp water
1 tbsp rose water
100g white chocolate,
  roughly chopped
3 tbsp freeze-dried
  raspberries
1 tbsp dried rose petals

This versatile dough is perfect for family cookie cutter fun with jammy fillings and beautifully hand-decorated creations for any occasion. In February we make these delicate heart shapes and sandwich them together with raspberry rose jam. Decorated with rose petals and white chocolate, they're perfect for that special someone in your life.

Preheat your oven to 190°C/170°C fan/gas 5.

Place the butter, sugar, salt and vanilla in a bowl or your stand mixer. Gently beat until creamed but not airy. Crack the eggs into a bowl and whisk lightly with a fork before gradually adding, taking care not to incorporate too much air. Lastly, add the flour in three additions, gently beating until a dough forms.

Tip the dough onto the counter and knead very briefly to make a block. Flour the counter and your rolling pin and take the dough down to 3mm thick. Cut out your heart shapes and lay on a couple of lined baking trays with space in between. Re-roll any offcuts, removing excess flour and gently pressing the dough together (over-kneading makes them tough).

Bake for 8–10 minutes, checking the cookies and turning the trays after 7 minutes. The colour should still be very pale and move slightly if pushed with your finger. Allow to cool completely on the trays, then turn half over.

Place the jam in a small saucepan with the water. Bring to the boil and simmer for a few minutes until thick, then stir in the rose water. Remove from the heat and place a dollop on the turned-over cookies. Leave to cool for a couple of minutes, then gently press the other cookies on top.

Place the chocolate in a small heatproof bowl that will fit over the top of a saucepan. Fill the pan with a small amount of water (making sure it won't touch the bottom of the bowl) and place the bowl of chocolate on top. Bring the water to a gentle simmer, allowing the chocolate to gradually melt, stirring every few minutes. White chocolate can seize (go grainy) easily, so make sure there is no contact with water or steam. Remove from the heat while there are still some unmelted pieces and continue to stir.

Use a piping bag or piece of baking parchment to make a small piping bag. Pipe lines of chocolate onto the cookies (or use a teaspoon to drizzle), then sprinkle on the raspberries and petals while the chocolate is still melted. Set before serving. These will keep in an airtight tin for up to 3 days or freeze in a covered container on the day of baking and store for 6 months.

GF

Amaretti cookies

Difficulty: ⬠
Makes: 14–16

Prep: 30 mins
Bake: 14–16 mins

500g ground almonds
50g light brown sugar
250g caster sugar
1 tsp baking powder
¼ tsp fine table salt
¼ tsp almond
 extract
180g egg whites or
 aquafaba
1 tsp lemon juice
100g icing sugar, sifted
100g flaked almonds

These little almond cookies are a result of my fascination with aquafaba (AKA chickpea water). This unlikely ingredient creates a stable foam with no discernible taste, making it a great vegan substitute for egg white. The popularity of these little treats soon outstripped our use for chickpeas, so we now source this amazing liquid from a local hummus producer.

To achieve the perfect combination of crisp and chewy takes a bit of practise, so keep a close eye on these cookies while they're baking – you're after a pale golden colour on the raised outer edges and on the tips of the flaked almonds in the centre. Too dark, and they'll be more crunch than chew.

Preheat the oven to 195°C/175°C fan/gas 5–6.

Weigh the ground almonds, brown and caster sugars, baking powder and salt into a large bowl. Add the almond extract and use a whisk to break up any lumps and distribute the almond flavouring.

Use a stand mixer or electric beaters to whip the egg white/aquafaba. Make sure the bowl and whisk attachment are clean and grease-free. Whisk on slow speed for the first couple of minutes, then increase the speed, add the lemon juice and whisk for 6–10 minutes until very stiff peaks have formed.

Fold a quarter of the foam into the dry mix using a scraper or spatula. Keep folding until all the dry matter is incorporated and there are no more lumps. Add the next quarter and continue to fold, becoming increasingly gentle as you add the last additions so you retain as much air as possible.

Portion the mix at 60g per cookie, gently forming into balls before rolling in the icing sugar. Place on a couple of lined baking sheets, spaced slightly apart. Push the flaked almonds firmly into the centre of each ball so that the tips of the almonds point upwards like a hedgehog. This flattens the centre of each cookie and creates their distinctive cracked crust. Dust the whole sheets generously with icing sugar just before baking.

Bake for 14–16 minutes, turning the sheets after 12 minutes. These will keep in an airtight tin for up to 3 days or freeze in a covered container on the day of baking and store for 6 months.

Summer berry friends

Difficulty: ⬚ ⬚
Makes: 10

. . . .

Prep: 30 mins
Rest: 2 hrs–overnight
Bake: 20–25 mins

. . . .

Equipment: 5cm
 cylindrical-shaped
 silicone moulds or
 a mini muffin tin

. . . .

130g unsalted butter
160g caster sugar
80g ground almonds
50g plain (or gluten-
 free) flour
130g egg whites
150g seasonal berries
 (or stone fruits, figs,
 rhubarb, chopped)
100g Raspberry Vanilla
 Jam (see page 239)
50g apricot jam, sieved
50g pistachios, roughly
 chopped

Fruity little almond cakes with a dollop of home-made jam in the centre – a great afternoon pick-me-up and a long-standing favourite with our customers. Choose seasonal fruit such as sharp summer berries, juicy plums or autumnal figs and blackberries. This recipe also works well with gluten-free flour.

Make the friand mix a couple of hours ahead (or even the day before) to allow the ground almonds to absorb the liquid egg white and melted butter – the firm batter will rise more evenly.

Brown the butter (see note on page 58) by bringing it to the boil in a pan. Allow it to bubble fiercely for 5–8 minutes, scraping the bottom of the pan with a spatula regularly. When the butter starts to smell sweet and nutty and the boiling foam rises up in the pan, pour the hot liquid (including the brown flecks and scrapings from the bottom of the pan) into a heatproof bowl. Allow the butter to cool, stirring occasionally as it firms up.

Weigh the sugar, ground almonds and flour into a bowl and whisk until combined. Still using the whisk, gradually add the egg whites, then the cooled browned butter in three stages until absorbed and no longer oily-looking. Cover the mix and leave to rest for a couple of hours or in the fridge overnight.

Preheat your oven to 180°C/160°C fan/gas 4.

Grease your mini cake moulds or muffin tin. Place half the fruit at the bottom of the moulds, then pipe or scoop your friand mix to come a third of the way up the sides. Use a small spoon to place the jam into the middle of each cake before topping with a dollop of the remaining batter. Your moulds will be about two-thirds full. Decorate with more fruit on top.

Bake for 20–25 minutes, turning the moulds or tin after 15 minutes. Use a skewer to check the cakes – it should come out clean. Cool for 5 minutes before removing from the moulds/tin and cooling on a rack.

Warm the sieved apricot jam and brush over the top of each cake, then sprinkle with the chopped pistachios.

Chocolate marmalade Bundt cakes

Difficulty: ▢▢
Makes: 12

Prep: 30 mins
Set: overnight
Bake: 25–30 mins
Cool: 15 minutes

Equipment: Small Bundt
  tin moulds or deep
  muffin tins

Day before: ganache
60g honey
60g caster sugar
60g unsalted butter,
  cubed
200g dark chocolate,
  roughly chopped
200ml double cream

Bake day: cakes
200g plain flour
50g ground almonds
1 tbsp ground cardamom
2 tsp baking powder
¼ tsp bicarbonate
  of soda
½ tsp fine sea salt
2 eggs
220g honey
30g plain yoghurt
150g dark chocolate
2 tbsp instant espresso
  coffee granules
100ml hot water
50g cocoa powder
200g marmalade
Zest and juice of 1 orange
100g unsalted butter

Marmalade, coffee and dark chocolate – deliciously rich bittersweet flavours. Use the chunkiest marmalade you can get your hands on or add crystallised orange peel if you're stuck with the thin stuff. Bundt tins are great if you've got them as the central hole fills with luscious chocolate ganache.

Make the ganache the day before to allow it to set. Place all the ingredients except the cream into a heatproof bowl. Warm the cream until just steaming, then pour into the bowl. Do not stir – allow to sit undisturbed for at least 5 minutes, then stir (or use a stick blender) to smooth the ganache, taking care not to incorporate any air. Cover the bowl and leave at room temperature overnight to set.

Preheat the oven to 180°C/160°C fan/gas 4.

Combine the flour, ground almonds, cardamom, baking powder, bicarbonate of soda and salt in a large bowl and whisk together. In a small bowl, mix the eggs, honey and yoghurt. Roughly chop your chocolate.

In another small bowl, add the espresso granules and hot water, then sift the cocoa powder over and mix to form a smooth paste. (You can use 60g strong espresso coffee instead – just reduce the hot water to 70ml).

In another small bowl, combine the marmalade, orange zest and juice and whisk to combine. Melt the butter in a small pan.

Make a well in the centre of the dry mix and pour in the egg mix, butter, coffee-cocoa mix, half the chocolate and half the marmalade mix. Stir the batter until smooth, stopping as soon as there are no more lumps of flour.

Grease then flour 12 Bundt tin moulds or 2 large muffin tins and pour in the batter. Bake for 25–30 minutes or until the cakes are pulling away from the sides. Check by inserting a skewer – it should come out clean.

Cool in the tins for 15 minutes, then remove and cool on a rack. Use a skewer to make holes in the cakes, then pour the remaining marmalade mix through a sieve (save the peel) and brush generously over the cakes.

Warm the chocolate ganache very slightly and gently pour over each cake. Decorate with pieces of orange peel and the remaining chopped chocolate.

(GF)

Black sesame and miso financiers

Difficulty: ▢ ▢
Makes: 10-12

....

Prep: 30 mins
Chill: 2 hrs–overnight
Bake: 14–16 mins

....

Equipment: Financier
mould/tin or 5cm
circular silicone or
metal moulds

....

35g black sesame
seeds, plus 1 tbsp extra
for decoration
160g unsalted butter
190g caster sugar
90g plain (or gluten-
free) flour
95g ground almonds
160g egg whites
(approx. 5 eggs)
50g tahini paste
1 tbsp miso paste,
plus 1 tsp for the glaze
1 tbsp white
sesame seeds
50ml water
50g Salted Caramel
Sauce (see page 259)

Traditionally made with almond flour, the name of these little cakes is said to originate from their popularity with bankers working at the French stock exchange as their shape is reminiscent of gold ingots. Fern, our genius bakery manager, created this little beauty with tahini and sesame seeds in the cake batter, followed by a miso caramel soak for a salty sweet umami taste.

Preheat the oven to 180°C/160°C fan/gas 4.

Roast the black sesame seeds for 10–12 minutes, then allow to cool. Grind the seeds in a small grinder until they form a paste.

Brown the butter (see note on page 58) by bringing it to the boil in a pan. Allow it to bubble fiercely for 5–8 minutes, scraping the bottom of the pan with a spatula regularly. When the butter starts to smell sweet and nutty and the boiling foam rises up in the pan, pour the hot liquid (including the brown flecks and scrapings from the bottom of the pan) into a heatproof bowl. Allow the butter to cool, stirring occasionally as it firms up.

Combine the sugar, flour and ground almonds in a large bowl, then pour in the egg whites slowly to combine all the ingredients. Add the tahini paste, black sesame and miso pastes. Slowly add the cooled brown butter, incorporating each addition fully before adding more. Place the batter in the fridge for several hours or overnight to chill.

Scoop the batter into the mould. It should come two-thirds of the way up the sides. Sprinkle with a mix of black and white sesame seeds. Bake for 14–16 minutes, turning the mould after 10 minutes. Allow to cool in the mould then remove.

Combine the water, caramel sauce and extra teaspoon of miso together in a pan and heat gently until warm to the touch. Dip each financier into the glaze, then set to dry out on a rack. Store in an airtight container for up to 1 week.

GF

Salted caramel and buttered almond brownies

Difficulty: 🍞
Makes: 16

Prep: 30 mins
Bake: 20-25 mins

Equipment: Digital thermometer

Salted caramel
50g unsalted butter
150g caster sugar
Generous pinch of
 flaky sea salt

Buttered almonds
120g whole almonds,
 skin on, roughly
 chopped
20g unsalted butter
½ tsp flaky sea salt

Brownie mix
150g unsalted butter
50g milk chocolate,
 roughly chopped
150g dark chocolate,
 roughly chopped
3 eggs
½ tsp vanilla extract
150g caster sugar
150g light brown sugar
80g cocoa powder
30g cornflour, sifted
½ tsp flaky sea salt, plus
 extra for sprinkling

Salted Caramel Sauce
 (see page 259), to
 serve (optional)

The devil's in the detail with a brownie. There are those that whisk until pale and voluminous, those that melt and fold, and those that beat the mix for a full minute until the batter is silky and shiny enough to create a crackly top and a dense, fudgy, intensely chocolatey interior (that's us). Our gluten-free recipe has been tweaked and honed over the years and we think it's pretty good. For the purist, leave out the nuts and caramel and spend your money on a single origin chocolate. We use a rich, fruity Madagascan for its deliciously distinctive taste.

To make the salted caramel, grease and line a shallow tin. In a heavy-based pan, gently melt the butter and sugar until the sugar is fully dissolved. Increase the heat and continue to boil until the caramel reaches 150°C (use a thermometer). Carefully pour into the tin and sprinkle with sea salt. Cool completely, then turn out and bash with a rolling pin to create shards.

Preheat the oven to 185°C/165°C fan/gas 4–5. Grease and line a 23cm x 23cm x 5cm square baking tin.

Put the almonds on a baking tray with the butter. Roast for 2 minutes so the butter melts, then remove and toss the nuts in the butter with the salt. Roast for 5–10 minutes until lightly toasted and smelling irresistible.

Make a bain-marie by selecting a heatproof bowl that is slightly larger than your saucepan. Fill the saucepan with an inch of water and place over a medium heat. Place the butter and chocolates in the bowl and set it on top of the pan so that it doesn't touch the water. Alternatively, use a microwave on full power in 30-second bursts. Remove before the chocolate is fully melted, then stir together until emulsified and leave to cool slightly.

Using a hand whisk, gently beat the eggs and vanilla with the sugars. In a separate bowl, combine your cocoa powder, sifted cornflour and salt. Using a spatula, gradually combine the chocolate mix with the egg, stirring in a figure-of-8, then add the dry ingredients in three stages. Continue to beat for a full minute until glossy and starting to pull away from the sides.

Pour into the tin, smoothing the top. Press the almonds and caramel into the batter, sprinkle with salt and bake for 20–25 minutes. Test for doneness with a skewer, avoiding pools of caramel – it should come out with a few damp crumbs stuck to it. If it's still liquid, give it 5 minutes more. Cool in the tin, then chill for 30 minutes. Serve with caramel sauce, if using.

Lemon shortbread bars

Difficulty: ☐ ☐
Makes: 12

....

Prep: 30 mins
Bake: 30–40 mins
Chill: 2 hrs–overnight

....

Shortbread base
170g plain (or gluten-
   free) flour
60g caster sugar
140g melted unsalted
   butter
½ tsp vanilla bean paste

Lemon filling
4 lemons, preferably
   unwaxed
300g caster sugar
40g cornflour
5 eggs
90g melted
   unsalted butter
Icing sugar, for dusting

Mouth-puckeringly sharp, this baked lemon curd on a crunchy shortbread base is best served chilled and prettily dusted with icing sugar. It's popular all year round with our customers – in fact, one of our regulars was so addicted to it she even underwent hypnosis to curb her craving (this is a true story!). This recipe works well with gluten-free flour, too.

Preheat the oven to 190°C/170°C fan/gas 5.

Start with the shortbread base, weighing your flour, sugar and a generous pinch of fine table salt into a bowl and whisking to combine. Gradually pour the melted butter onto the dry ingredients and add the vanilla, mixing with a spatula until it clumps together to form a rough dough (or use a stand mixer with the paddle attachment on slow speed).

Press the dough evenly into a greased and lined 23cm x 23cm x 5cm square baking tin (if you're using a loose-bottomed tin make sure it's fully lined so the liquid mix doesn't seep out). Bake for 10–15 minutes until firm and dry to the touch, though still very pale in colour. Remove and fully cool.

Reduce the oven temperature to 175°C/155°C fan/gas 3–4.

Wash the lemons thoroughly. Slice two of the lemons into rings, 3mm thick, and remove the pips. Place the slices into a blender and grind to a pulp. Add the sugar and cornflour and continue until you have a fine purée. Juice the remaining two lemons and add this juice to the blender along with the eggs, melted butter and a generous pinch of salt. Pulse briefly to combine.

Place the tin with the shortbread base into your oven, keeping the door open. Carefully pour the lemon mix over the shortbread base and bake for 20–25 minutes until firm. The lemon layer should be set but not browned.

Cool, then chill in the fridge. Once firm, carefully remove from the tin, dust heavily with icing sugar and cut into bars.

Pear, sage and almond cake

Difficulty: ⏹⏹
Serves: 12

....

Prep: 30 mins
Bake: 45–55 mins

....

Base layer
150g soft unsalted butter
75g light brown sugar
150g plain flour
50g semolina or rice
  flour, finely ground
¼ tsp fine sea salt

Frangipane layer
135g light brown sugar
135g soft unsalted butter
2 eggs
1 tsp vanilla bean paste
50g plain flour
135g ground almonds
½ tsp baking powder
10g fresh sage, finely
  chopped
½ recipe Vanilla Custard
  Base (see page 254),
  chilled

Fruit layer
3 Conference pears,
  peeled
Unsalted butter, for
  brushing
Icing sugar, for
  sprinkling
¼ tsp flaky sea salt

To finish
2 tbsp Salted Caramel
  Sauce (see page 259)
Fresh sage leaves
10g unsalted butter

This recipe is endlessly adaptable. Choose whatever fruit looks irresistible in your greengrocers and pair it with fresh herbs or spices. We love shocking pink rhubarb with ginger in springtime and peaches, raspberries and fennel in summer. It would also be great with gooseberries and elderflower, plums, blackberries and star anise . . . I could go on. A very versatile addition to your repertoire.

Folding pastry cream into frangipane keeps everything light and moist, while the crisp shortbread base gives structure to each slice.

Preheat the oven to 200°C/180°C fan/gas 6. Grease and line a 23cm x 23cm x 5cm square baking tin.

For the base, beat the butter and sugar on slow speed until softened but not aerated. Add the flour, semolina and salt, then continue beating on slow until it comes together. Don't overmix. Press the shortbread into the tin, smoothing down, then prick it all over with a fork. Bake for 20–25 minutes until pale golden brown and dry to the touch. Cool.

Make the frangipane by beating the sugar and butter together until light and fluffy. Add the eggs, one at a time, and beat until fully incorporated. Add the vanilla. Weigh the plain flour, ground almonds and baking powder into a bowl and whisk to combine, then add to the egg mix and beat briefly on slow speed to combine. Add the sage, then fold the chilled pastry cream into the frangipane in three additions.

Spread the frangipane over the shortbread base. Slice the pears in half from tip to base, then again into quarters. Remove the core and slice into eighths. Lay the pears onto the frangipane, brush lightly with a little melted butter, then sprinkle over a little icing sugar and the salt. Bake for 25–30 minutes until the pears are lightly caramelised and the frangipane is golden brown, turning the tin after 15 minutes.

Leave to cool in the tin before removing, then warm the caramel sauce and drizzle over the surface. Sprinkle with the sage leaves, first lightly fried in the butter to crisp up. Serve with a dollop of crème fraîche.

Strawberry rhubarb tart with black pepper and balsamic

Difficulty: ☐ ☐ ☐
Serves: 8–10

Prep: 45 mins
Chill: 30 mins
Blind baking: 35 mins
Bake: 30–40 mins

Equipment: 25cm loose-
   bottomed tart tin
   Baking beans

½ recipe Flaky Pastry
   (see page 251)

Black pepper frangipane
100g caster sugar
100g soft unsalted butter
2 eggs
50g plain flour
125g ground almonds
2 tsp black pepper

Fruit topping
400g rhubarb
300g strawberries
50g caster sugar
30g cornflour

To finish
2 tbsp balsamic vinegar
2 tbsp strawberry jam

When I first paired these fruits I was convinced the assertive rhubarb would overpower the delicate strawberry. Not so – in fact it, turns out that strawberry is the dominant flavour. This is a great way to use late season greeny-red rhubarb – the colour from the strawberries keeps everything gorgeously pink.

Grease the tart tin well. Roll the cold pastry into a disc 3–5mm thick, making quarter turns as you roll, until it's approx. 5cm wider than the base of the tin. Using your rolling pin, lift and gently lay the pastry over the tin with an even overhang. Working your way round, use one hand to lift and support the pastry while pressing downwards on the inner edge with your other hand. This ensures the pastry isn't stretched and won't shrink back when you blind bake the tart case. Don't trim the pastry edges, just let it drape over the edge of the tin while it bakes. Prick the base with a fork and chill for at least 30 minutes in the fridge (or 10 minutes in the freezer).

Preheat your oven to 200°C/180°C fan/gas 6.

Line the chilled pastry case with cling film or baking parchment, draping it over the edges of the tin. Fill with baking beans and bake for 20 minutes, then remove from the oven. Remove the plastic/paper and beans and bake for another 10–15 minutes until the pastry looks dry and light golden. Remove from the oven and allow to cool fully, then use a knife or microplane grater to remove the excess pastry.

To make the frangipane, beat the sugar and butter until smooth, then add the eggs, one by one. Combine the flour, ground almonds and pepper in a bowl, then gradually add to the egg mix. Smooth this over the cooled pastry shell.

Cut the rhubarb into 1cm sections and slice large strawberries in half. Toss in a bowl with the sugar and cornflour. Pile the fruit on top of the frangipane and bake for 30–40 minutes until the frangipane is golden brown and the fruit lightly caramelised. Remove from the oven and cool.

In a small pan, combine the balsamic with the jam and a generous splash of water, bring to a simmer, then brush over the tart. Don't allow it to become too thick or it will caramelise. Add a generous grind of black pepper to taste. Serve cold in thin slices with a dollop of crème fraîche.

Eccles cakes

Difficulty: ⬜ ⬜ ⬜
Makes: 13

Prep: 45 mins
Soak: overnight
Bake: 25–30 mins

Equipment: 10cm
round cutter

150g currants
100g raisins
½ tsp orange zest
¼ tsp lemon zest
2 tbsp orange juice
1 tbsp lemon juice
1 tsp brandy
¼ tsp fine sea salt
½ tsp ground cinnamon
1 tsp grated nutmeg
¼ tsp mixed spice
60g unsalted butter
90g light brown sugar
½ recipe (500g) Puff
  Pastry (see page 250)
30g egg white (1 egg),
  lightly beaten
2 tbsp demerara sugar

While these citrus-infused raisin and currant puff pastries are baking, the molten butter and sugar bubbles up through the cuts in the top, forming pools of deliciously spiced toffee. If possible, soak the fruit overnight and you can even bake from frozen – just add 5 minutes.

The day before, weigh the currants, raisins, orange and lemon zest and juice, brandy, salt and all the spices into a heatproof bowl. Place the butter and sugar in a heavy-based pan and gently heat, stirring regularly for about 5 minutes until the sugar is dissolved. Pour over the fruit and mix thoroughly. Allow to cool, stirring regularly for a few hours, then cover and refrigerate overnight.

The next day, preheat your oven to 220°C/200°C fan/gas 7.

Lightly flour your counter and roll out your pastry to approx. 40cm x 30cm. Use the cutter to cut out 12 discs, approx. 3mm thick. Stack up your offcuts (keep the layers running in the same direction) and re-roll to get a 'not quite perfect' bonus disc – just let the dough relax fully before you cut it out.

Use your hands to firmly press the fruit into 40–50g balls and place each ball onto a pastry disc. Carefully lift the opposite sides of the circle and pinch together, then do the same with the other sides. Firmly pinch any remaining pastry into the centre so the filling is completely enclosed. Gently tap on the counter to seal underneath. Place onto a lined baking tray, slightly spaced apart, and brush with egg white. Sprinkle on a little demerara sugar, then make a few slits about 1cm long with a sharp knife in the top of each pastry.

Bake for 20 minutes, then turn the tray and bake for 5–10 minutes until crisp and golden. Best on the day they're made or keep in an airtight tin for 3 days.

Eccles cakes with Lancashire cheese

I love Lancashire cheese. Sharp and crumbly with a gentle zesty flavour. As a small child, I remember visiting the cheese counters at Lancaster indoor market with my gran. The air was different – cold and damp with a sharp lactic tang. At our regular counter the lady would lean over and offer me Lancashire crumbly, speared on the tip of a knife. Fear of the blade was tempered with a desire not to waste a single crumb as I carefully removed the little cube and popped it in my mouth. It's a Northern tradition to pair it with a wedge of fruitcake or jam, so here's a little play on that. Make your fruit mix portions slightly smaller and dice Lancashire cheese into 13 x 10g pieces. Press the fruit mix around the cheese, enclose inside a pastry disc, then bake.

Salted caramel tart with torched meringue

Difficulty: ◻ ◻
Serves: 6–10

Prep: 1 hr
Chill: 30 mins + setting
Blind baking: 30 mins

Equipment: 20cm loose-
bottomed tart tin
Baking beans
Piping bag with a
1.5cm round tip
Blowtorch (optional)

½ recipe (approx. 380g)
Chocolate Sweet
Pastry (see page 249)
1 egg
3 tbsp Salted Caramel
Sauce (see page 259)
1 x Italian Meringue (see
page 256)

Ganache
300g dark chocolate,
chopped
50g unsalted butter,
cut into small cubes
1 tbsp glucose or
golden syrup
300ml double cream

Inspired by the campfire treat s'mores (some more, geddit?), this tart is layers of pure indulgence. It works equally well with our usual sweet pastry, but chocolate contrasts wonderfully with the toasty meringue.

Grease the tart tin and line the base with a disc of baking parchment. Lightly flour the counter and your rolling pin and roll the chilled pastry out to approx. 3–5mm thick, making quarter turns as you roll, until it's approx. 5cm wider than the base of the tin. Using your rolling pin, lift and gently lay the pastry over the tin with an even overhang. Working your way round, use one hand to lift and support the pastry while pressing downwards on the inner edge with your other hand. This ensures the pastry isn't stretched and won't shrink back when you bake. Use a rolling pin across the edge of the tin to cut off excess pastry, prick the base with a fork and refrigerate for at least 30 minutes (or 10 minutes in the freezer) with the leftover trimmings.

Preheat the oven to 210°C/190°C fan/gas 6–7.

Line the chilled pastry case with cling film or baking parchment, draping it over the edges of the tin. Fill with baking beans and bake for 25 minutes, then remove from the oven. Carefully lift out the plastic/paper and beans and allow to cool slightly. Beat the egg lightly, brush over the pastry base, then place back in the oven for 5 minutes until crisp. Place the trimmings on another tray and bake along with the case until crisp (10–15 minutes).

Warm the caramel sauce slightly, then pour over the pastry base, allowing it to spread to the edges. Remove the case from the tin once fully cooled.

Prepare the ganache by placing the chocolate, butter and syrup in a heatproof bowl. Heat the cream until steaming, then pour over. Leave to stand, undisturbed, for 5 minutes, then stir to combine. Cool slightly before pouring over the cooled tart case and placing in the fridge to set.

Fill your piping bag (or snip off the end of a disposable piping bag) with the cooled Italian meringue. Starting from the centre, pipe peaks of meringue over the surface of the tart, pulling the bag upwards as you pipe to create elongated tips.

Use a blowtorch (or place briefly under a hot grill) to toast the surface. Crush the pastry trimmings until fine, then sprinkle over the finished tart for some extra crunch, if desired.

Chocolate amaretto tart

Difficulty: 🍞 🍞
Serves: 6–10

Prep: 40 mins + cooling
Chill: 30 mins + setting
Blind baking: 30 mins
Bake: 30–35 mins

Equipment: 20cm loose-
bottomed tart tin
Baking beans

½ recipe (approx. 380g)
   Chocolate Sweet
   Pastry (see page 249)
1 egg

Tart filling
180g dark chocolate,
   chopped
120g unsalted butter
35g caster sugar
1 egg
20g egg yolk (1 egg)
80ml amaretto liqueur
½ tsp almond extract

To decorate
30g flaked almonds
Icing sugar

The perfect bake-ahead dessert for when you want to impress, ideal served with a dollop of crème fraîche and a small glass of amaretto to finish a special meal. This tart also works well with Cherry Amaretto Jam (see page 236) spread generously over the blind-baked pastry case before filling with chocolate batter. Press a fresh cherry, complete with stalk, into each 'slice' before baking and dredge with icing sugar.

Grease the tart tin and line the base with a disc of baking parchment. Lightly flour the counter and your rolling pin and roll the chilled pastry out to approximately 3–5mm thick, making quarter turns as you roll, until it's approx. 5cm wider than the base of the tin. Using your rolling pin, lift and gently lay the pastry over the tin with an even overhang. Working your way round, use one hand to lift and support the pastry while pressing downwards on the inner edge with your other hand. This ensures the pastry isn't stretched and won't shrink back when you bake. Use a rolling pin across the edge of the tin to cut off excess pastry, prick the base with a fork and refrigerate for at least 30 minutes (or 10 minutes in the freezer).

Preheat the oven to 210°C/190°C fan/gas 6–7.

Line the chilled pastry case with cling film or baking parchment, draping it over the edges of the tin. Fill with baking beans and bake for 25 minutes, then remove from the oven. Carefully lift out the plastic/paper and beans and allow to cool slightly. Beat the egg lightly, brush over the pastry base, then place back in the oven for 5 minutes until crisp.

Reduce the oven temperature to 190°C/170°C fan/gas 5.

Make a bain-marie with a heatproof bowl slightly larger than your saucepan. Fill the pan with an inch of water and place over a medium heat. Place the chocolate and butter in the bowl and set it on top of the saucepan, so that it doesn't touch the water. Alternatively, use a microwave on full power in 30-second bursts. Remove before the chocolate is fully melted, then stir.

In a stand mixer or using electric beaters, whisk the sugar, egg and yolk together until pale and thick, then gently fold the chocolate mix into the egg mix, followed by the amaretto and the almond extract.

Fill the case with the batter and sprinkle the almonds over the surface. Bake for 30–35 minutes until the tart has risen very slightly with a firm wobble. Cool, then chill the tart before serving with a sprinkle of icing sugar.

Luscious lemon tart

Difficulty: ⬚⬚
Serves: 6–10

....

Prep: 1 hr
Blind baking: 30 mins
Chill: 30 mins + setting

....

Equipment: 20cm loose-bottomed tart tin
Baking beans

....

½ recipe Sweet
   Pastry (see page 248)
4 eggs
190ml lemon juice
190g caster sugar
60g egg yolks (3 eggs)
190g unsalted butter,
   cubed
3 small leaves of
   gelatine (Dr Oetker
   brand) or 1 tsp agar
   agar powder
   (vegetarian alternative)

To decorate
Meringues Kisses (see
   page 256)
Candied Lemon Peel or
   slices (see page 257)
Fresh berries and
   redcurrants

A popular option in our celebration cake range, this tart makes a lovely centrepiece on a summer table finished with luscious berries. Place the meringues on the tart just before serving so they retain their crunch or paint the base of each kiss with melted white chocolate to 'waterproof' it. The lemon curd-style filling is set with gelatine (with a vegetarian option), making it easy to slice.

Grease the tart tin and line the base with a disc of baking parchment. Lightly flour the counter and your rolling pin and roll the chilled pastry out to approximately 3–5mm thick, making quarter turns as you roll, until it's approx. 5cm wider than the base of the tin. Using your rolling pin, lift and gently lay the pastry over the tin with an even overhang. Working your way round, use one hand to lift and support the pastry while pressing downwards on the inner edge with your other hand. This ensures the pastry isn't stretched and won't shrink back when you bake. Use a rolling pin across the edge of the tin to cut off excess pastry, prick the base with a fork and refrigerate for at least 30 minutes (or 10 minutes in the freezer).

Preheat the oven to 210°C/190°C fan/gas 6–7.

Line the chilled pastry case with cling film or baking parchment, draping it over the edges of the tin. Fill with baking beans and bake for 25 minutes, then remove from the oven. Carefully lift out the plastic/paper and beans and allow to cool slightly. Beat one egg lightly, brush over the pastry base, then place back in the oven for 5 minutes until crisp.

Make a bain-marie by selecting a heatproof bowl that is slightly larger than your saucepan. Fill the pan with an inch of water and place over a medium heat. Place the lemon juice, sugar, remaining whole eggs, the egg yolks and cubed butter in the bowl and set it on top of the pan, so that it doesn't touch the water. If you're using the agar agar powder, add that now, too. Heat gently, stirring, until the curd is thick enough to coat the back of a spoon. Remove from the heat.

If using gelatine, soak in cold water for 5 minutes, then wring out to remove excess water. Stir the gelatine into the hot lemon mix until dissolved.

Pour the lemon curd into the tart case and refrigerate for a couple of hours to set. Decorate with meringue kisses, candied lemon peel and fresh berries.

Dreamy apple cake

Difficulty: ⬜ ⬜
Serves: 8–10

Prep: 1 hr
Bake: 45 mins–1 hr

Equipment: 20cm
 deep cake tin
 Piping bag with a
 3cm plain nozzle

Apple cake
4 Bramley apples
2 tsp lemon juice
3 eggs
180g caster sugar
1 tsp vanilla extract
½ tsp fine sea salt
180ml neutral oil
240g plain flour
1½ tsp baking powder
1 tsp ground cinnamon

Crumble topping
50g unsalted butter
100g plain flour
50g caster sugar
1 tsp ground cinnamon

Apple filling
100g Bramley apples
65g caster sugar

Caramel icing
320g mascarpone
80g cream cheese
 (Philadelphia)
20g icing sugar
100g Salted Caramel
 Sauce (see page 259),
 plus extra for the top
160ml double cream

Working that classic bonfire night combination of toffee and apple, this tall, multi-layered cake is filled with tart Bramley apples and a dreamy caramel icing.

Preheat the oven to 195°C/175°C fan/gas 5–6 and grease and line the cake tin with baking parchment.

Peel and core the apples, then cut into 1cm cubes. Place in a bowl and toss in the lemon juice. Beat the eggs, caster sugar, vanilla and sea salt by hand (or using a stand mixer with the beater attachment or electric beaters on a medium speed) until light and foamy – about 5 minutes. Gradually add the neutral oil, allowing it to be incorporated before the next addition.

In a separate bowl, whisk together the flour, baking powder and cinnamon. Fold the dry ingredients into the wet mix in three additions, taking care not to overmix. Lastly, fold in the apple and pour into the tin. Bake for 45 minutes–1 hour, turning the tin after 30 minutes. Remove when a skewer inserted into the centre of the cake comes out clean. Cool in the tin.

While the cake is baking, make the topping. Rub the butter into the flour and stir in the sugar, cinnamon and a pinch of salt. Press into a lined tray and bake for 10–15 minutes until golden. Cool, then break into chunks.

Peel and core the Bramleys, then roughly chop. Add to a small pan with the sugar and a splash of water. Simmer gently with the lid on until the apple has started to collapse and form a dry, chunky compote. Cool before using.

Prepare the icing by beating together the mascarpone, cream cheese, icing sugar, caramel sauce and a pinch of sea salt. In a separate bowl, whip the double cream until it is holding soft peaks, then fold it into the cheese mix.

Once the cake is cool, cut it into three even layers. Place the bottom layer onto a cake board. Place two-thirds of the caramel icing into a piping bag with a 3cm plain nozzle and pipe a series of concentric rings from the centre to the outer edge around the bottom layer of cake. Smooth to create an even layer, then pipe a second ring around the outer edge – this will retain the apple filling. Fill the central area with half the apple filling.

Place the next cake layer on top and repeat the icing rings and apple. Place the top layer of cake on top of the second layer. Finally, use the remaining icing to thinly cover the sides (don't worry if you don't have full coverage) and decorate the top with extra caramel sauce and a sprinkling of crumble.

Adnams Broadside bread pudding

Difficulty: ⭕
Makes: 12

Prep: 45 mins
Bake: 30 mins

Equipment: 23cm x 23cm x 5cm tin

500g Classic Magpie Sourdough (see page 137)
300g currants
40g mixed peel
1 tbsp orange zest
180g caster sugar
200ml boiling water
2 strong teabags
120g unsalted butter, cubed
100ml double cream
200ml dark ale
70g plain flour
1 tsp baking powder
1 tbsp mixed spice
3 eggs
2 tbsp demerara sugar

When you're running a bakery, it's hard to predict how much bread to make each day so this recipe started life as a necessity. We use dark and malty Adnams Broadside beer, but any tasty local brew will work. At Christmas we give this recipe a little twist, adding cardamom, cinnamon and flecks of dark chocolate and serving it warm with brandy cream.

Cut the hard crusts from the bread and chop the bread into 3cm cubes. Place the cubed bread into a large bowl and add the currants, mixed peel, orange zest and caster sugar.

Boil the kettle and make a pot of strong tea. Brew, then add the required amount to the bread mix.

Add the butter to a small pan and pour in the cream. Stir together once the butter is melted and add to the bread mix along with the beer. Stir to combine.

In a separate bowl, whisk together the flour, baking powder and mixed spice, then add to the bread mix in three additions, making sure there are no lumps of dry flour. Finally, add the eggs and mix thoroughly to combine. Pour into a greased tin, pressing down gently to create an even surface.

Preheat the oven to 195°C/175°C fan/gas 5–6 while allowing the mix to rest for 15 minutes to fully absorb the liquid.

Sprinkle heavily with demerara sugar just before placing in the oven. Bake for 30 minutes, turning the tin after 20 minutes. The bread pudding is ready when a skewer comes out clean. Cool in the tin, then cut into slices.

Tiramisu layer cake

Difficulty: ⬜ ⬜
Serves: 8–10

Prep: 1 hr

**Equipment: Piping bag
with a 1.5cm round tip**

Vanilla Genoise
Cakes (see page 252)
100g cocoa powder,
sifted

Coffee syrup
3 tsp instant espresso
coffee granules
120ml boiling water
(or 130ml strong
espresso coffee)
120g caster sugar

Marsala cream icing
250g mascarpone
130ml double cream
130g icing sugar
45ml Marsala

Tiramisu was the only dessert on the menu at a wonderful pizzeria I visited in Florence and was deservedly popular. Sometimes I think we forget just how good the classics are so here, in cake form, I give you a layered genoise sponge soaked in coffee syrup – the perfect foil for a rich Marsala mascarpone icing dredged in bitter cocoa.

Prepare the coffee syrup using either coffee granules and hot water or hot espresso coffee. Add the sugar and stir to dissolve.

Using a whisk, beat the mascarpone until smooth and thick, then add the cream, icing sugar and Marsala. Beat until thick and holding soft peaks.

Slice the two genoise cakes in half so you have four layers. Level the top cake layers and place one on the cake board to use as the base. Brush with the coffee syrup.

Reserve 200g of the Marsala icing to use on the top and sides of the cake. Spread a third of the remaining Marsala icing over the bottom layer of cake, then sift a generous layer of cocoa powder over the surface.

Repeat the cake, coffee syrup, Marsala icing and cocoa powder layers twice more, then place the final cake layer on top and use the remaining coffee syrup to brush over the top of the cake.

Smooth half of the reserved icing onto the sides and top of the cake, then pipe 'kisses' of Marsala icing over the cake's surface. Dredge the whole cake generously with cocoa powder.

Raspberry bloom cake

Difficulty: ⭕ ⭕ ⭕
Serves: 8–10

Prep: 1½ hrs
Bake: 25–30 mins
Chill: 2 hrs

Equipment: 2 x 20cm
   loose-bottomed
   cake tins
   Piping bag and 1cm
   round tip
   Cake turntable
   (optional)

525g plain flour
20g baking powder
4 eggs
400g caster sugar
480g sour cream
2 tsp vanilla extract
¾ tsp fine sea salt
225ml neutral oil
340g Raspberry Vanilla
   Jam (see page 239)

Italian meringue
buttercream
2 x Italian Meringue
   (see page 256)
440g soft unsalted
   butter

To decorate
Fresh flowers
Large punnet of
   berries or other fruit

This semi-naked cake, filled with jam and decorated with meringue buttercream, berries and seasonal flowers, is a real showstopper. Piping the icing onto the cake layers, rather than spooning it, will ensure it's level and even for a professional finish. Thanks to Fern Harman and her team for working on this one.

Preheat your oven to 195°C/175°C fan/gas 5–6. Prepare your cake tins by greasing and lining the bases.

Weigh the flour and baking powder in a bowl and sift twice. Whisk the eggs and sugar using a stand mixer or electric beaters until pale and thick – this may take up to 10 minutes. Switch to the beater attachment and add the sour cream, vanilla and salt, then gradually stream in the oil. Fold in the flour mix in three additions – don't overmix or the cake will be tough!

Pour into the tins and bake for 20 minutes. Turn the tins and bake for another 5–10 minutes until each cake is pulling away from the sides of the tin and a skewer inserted into the centre comes out clean. Cool for 30 minutes, then remove from the tins and continue cooling on a rack.

While the cakes are baking, make the Italian meringue, whisking until the meringue is cool, thick and glossy. Add the butter gradually in small 1cm cubes, in three stages, whisking well between each addition, then beat for a further 5 minutes until voluminous and pale. Fill your piping bag using a 1cm round tip (or snip off the end of a disposable piping bag).

To decorate, level off both cakes by removing the top domed section. You can nibble on this to keep your energy levels up or dry and use as a decorative crumble in the future. Cut each sponge in half across the middle. I find the best way to achieve an even cut is to take my eye down to the same level as my knife (and cake) and as you cut, watch that both layers of the cake stay the same depth.

Dab a little buttercream onto a cake board or plate to secure the first layer – placing your cake board on a cake turntable if you have one. Use the bottom layer of a cake as your base layer, then keep the other bottom layer to use as the top layer. This will keep your layers even.

continued overleaf

Starting in the centre of the first layer, pipe a spiral of buttercream until you reach the edge, then smooth this over with a palette knife. Next, pipe another ring around the edge of the first layer and fill inside this with jam. Place the next cake layer on top. Repeat this a further two times, ending with the top layer of the cake, bottom side up. Gently push down on the cake and chill for 1 hour. Keep your remaining buttercream soft.

Once the cake is chilled, pipe a spiral of buttercream on the top, starting from the middle and working outwards. With a jug of hot water close by, use your palette knife to smooth out this layer. Apply pressure to scrape the icing back towards the cake.

Roughly pipe your buttercream evenly over the sides of the cake, piping more than you need on the upper section – don't worry how it looks. Using your palette knife in a back-and-forth motion, spread the icing around the sides of the cake. Next, hold the palette knife vertically against the cake and scrape around the sides in a few sweeping motions; once the cake is smooth, chill for another hour.

When the buttercream is firm, use a sharp knife dipped in hot water to cut the raised top edge of the cake by holding your knife flat to the horizontal surface while spinning the turntable or turning your cake plate. Finally, use a hot palette knife to smooth out any surface imperfections on top.

Select the prettiest seasonal flowers (remove non-edible flowers before serving) and fresh berries to decorate your cake.

Your
Daily
Bread

Think of breadmaking as your superpower – simple ingredients transformed into much more than the sum of their (four) parts. To perform this alchemy, you'll need time (the dough's, not necessarily yours), patience and the application of your growing knowledge. Bread is problem-solving, one bake at a time. Applying your hands, eyes and brain simultaneously is a great mental and physical workout. It slows you down as you become more present in the moment; days are measured by the stages of fermentation, shaping and baking. Perfect stress relief!

Adapting to the seasons or your ingredients means that baking bread is never repetitive, always rewarding and sometimes challenging.

This chapter is about 'good' bread – that's what I call bread that looks and tastes great, is easily digestible, keeps well and uses ingredients 'your grandmother would recognise' (to paraphrase Michael Pollen). At Two Magpies, our bread is predominantly made from a wild yeast culture – this bread is known as sourdough. When we use baker's yeast, we still want the health and flavour benefits of long-fermented dough, so we only use very small amounts. To this we add locally milled flour, water and some salt for flavour. That's it. Sometimes we like to add flavourful ingredients such as seeds, nuts, herbs or cheese but with bread that'll only get you so far – it's time that really makes the difference. As lactic and acetic acids build in the dough, bacteria work to fully break down carbohydrates and gluten – making it easier to digest, nutrients more bioavailable and, most importantly, taste delicious.

We all lead busy lives and dedicating your well-earned free time to breadmaking may seem like a big ask – in fact, it puts lots of people off baking in the first place. Yes, good bread does take time – but it doesn't need to be your time. Using the long fermentation methods in this book will leave you free to get on with your day with just a few minutes needed to observe, fold and shape over a few hours. Before you know it, you'll be baking smart and letting your fridge do the heavy lifting.

To the uninitiated, 'good' bread might seem a lot of fuss about nothing but since the introduction of the Chorleywood breadmaking process in the 1960s, this basic foodstuff has seen some dark times. If eating mass-produced bread with a long ingredients list leaves you feeling uncomfortable and bloated and you're not suffering from a recognised medical condition, your intolerance may not be to gluten but to industrialised bread processing. Many of these loaves contain large amounts of yeast to raise the bread quickly (sometimes just a couple of hours from flour sack to bagging), extra gluten in powdered form to compensate for poor-quality flour, improvers and 'allowable' additives that under current legislation don't have to be declared.

Long-fermented bread processes allow time for bacteria to fully break down carbohydrates and gluten, releasing the nutrients within and making it easier to digest. We regularly meet amazed 'gluten-intolerant' customers who enjoy our bread without digestive side effects.

Starting with some basic technical info, this section kicks off with a quick-and-easy soda bread recipe before moving on to yeasted and sourdough breads. Use the loaf symbol as a guide to assess the technical difficulty of each recipe.

Oh, and if you're wanting to tackle sourdough, remember you'll need at least a week's head start, so turn to page 131.

Breadmaking techniques

The world of breadmaking can seem a little impenetrable, especially if you find yourself down a Google black hole being bombarded with technical terminology. Suffice to say, I've kept the following section to the minimum required for the novice to make great bread, whilst giving enough detail to make sure you've set yourself up for success and can troubleshoot if necessary.

Calculating your water temperature

The desired dough temperature (DDT) for most doughs is 26°C. At this temperature, yeast (wild or baker's) is active and controllable. Above 26°C, fermentation will be fast, hard to control and without the health and flavour benefits of long fermentation. Below 26°C, fermentation is sluggish and your dough may be underproved and inconsistent.

To achieve the DDT you'll need to adjust the temperature of the water you're using so that it compensates for the air temperature in your kitchen. In winter, when the temperature in your kitchen is below 26°C, the water for your dough will need to be warmer to achieve a DDT of 26°C. In the height of summer, when your kitchen (and ingredient) temperature might be above 26°C, your water will need to be cooler (or even cold) to achieve the DDT. You'll find it's much easier to start with your dough at the correct temperature than to try and change it later. Try to maintain 26°C throughout the bulk fermentation, checking with each fold and responding accordingly.

DESIRED DOUGH TEMPERATURE (DDT) = 26°C

26 x 2 = 52

Example air temperature in your kitchen = 21°C

52 – 21 = 31°C (in this example your water temperature would be 31°C)

To make your water the right temperature, run the hot tap and half-fill a jug. Using a thermometer, add hotter or colder water depending on the temperature required and how much water you need. You'll be weighing your water using the scales so if you make a little extra it won't matter.

Preferment

Long-fermented bread has better flavour, digestibility and an extended shelf life. A preferment is simply a way to kick-start the fermentation process 12–18 hours before the main dough is mixed, similar to what we do with sourdough bread. Flour, water, a very small amount of yeast and a pinch of salt (to slow things down) creates a bubbly batter-like consistency full of yeasty acidity and bacteria, which is then added to the main dough. It's quick to make – you just need a spoon, scales and a bowl.

Autolyse

When flour and water are briefly mixed to form a rough dough, then left for approximately 30 minutes (or longer for wholemeal flours), it's referred to as the autolyse. Using this method will massively reduce your kneading time. The autolyse is a magic time and it will totally change the way you make bread.

WHAT'S ACTUALLY HAPPENING?

The hydrated flour molecules swell, causing enzymes within the grain to become active and start breaking down starches, making sugars available for the yeast when it's introduced later. Simultaneously, the proteins, gluten and gliadin are unlocked and start to develop a network of long-chain protein bonds that make the dough stronger, smoother and more extensible – all happening without any effort on your part!

Kneading

All the doughs in this book become strong and elastic through a combination of resting, gentle kneading (hand or machine) and stretching and folding. When it comes to making bread at home, I prefer the simplicity of a large bowl and a plastic scraper over a mixer. Once you find your rhythm, you'll find kneading incredibly satisfying and relaxing – almost meditative – and with the right action it doesn't have to be ridiculously hard work. Handling the dough keeps you, literally, in touch with what's going on and you'll feel it changing from sticky to smooth, weak to elastic and strong. Even if you're wedded to your mixer, have a go at hand kneading at least once.

1. After the first rest, turn your dough out onto an un-floured surface. The dough will feel sticky – don't panic and add more flour. Use your scraper to regularly bring the dough back together into one lump. The stickiness creates tension as you stretch and turn, stopping it slip-sliding around.

2. Lightly anchor the piece of dough closest to your body with the fingertips of your non-dominant hand, then push the heel of your dominant hand into the top portion of the dough and stretch it away from you to arm's length **(1)**.

3. At full stretch, curl your fingers around the top of the dough **(2)**.

4. Lift the dough upwards and back towards you, folding it over on itself **(3)**.

5. Give the dough a quarter turn anticlockwise with your non-dominant hand after every stretch/fold to keep changing your angle of attack. Repeat this movement for 5–8 minutes, setting a lively pace to keep the dough on the move. Resist the temptation to add more flour as you knead.

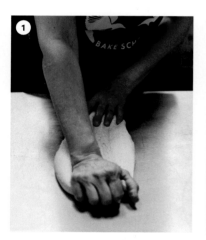 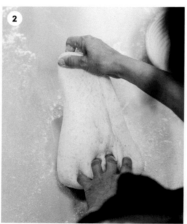 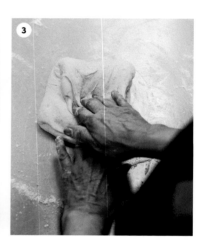

Windowpane test

Use the windowpane test regularly while kneading and during bulk fermentation to help you understand the qualities of the flour you're working with and how quickly it is developing a strong gluten network.

1. After letting the dough relax for a minute, delicately pinch a walnut-sized piece between the fingers and thumbs of both hands and gently extend it away from the larger mass of the dough.

2. The aim is to see how far you can stretch the thin 'windowpane' of dough before it tears (see opposite).

NO GLUTEN DEVELOPMENT
The dough looks lumpy, sticky and tears immediately when gently stretched.

MODERATE GLUTEN DEVELOPMENT
The dough looks smoother and stronger and can be stretched to a moderate level of transparency when stretched.

FULL GLUTEN DEVELOPMENT
The dough is smooth and strong and can be stretched considerably to the point of transparency, when you can see the colour of your skin underneath (see photo).

Bulk fermentation

Bulk fermentation is when the proving dough is 'bulked' together in the same bowl and not divided into individual loaves. This first proving can last from 3–5 hours ambient or overnight in the fridge.

Ambient bulk fermentation

This requires the dough to be around 26°C. During the ambient bulk fermentation, the dough is regularly folded to redistribute the temperature and build strength.

Cold bulk fermentation

This usually comes after a short period of ambient fermentation. It's a way of extending the breadmaking process either for flavour or convenience. The dough is kept in the fridge overnight and then shaped and further proved the following day.

WHAT'S ACTUALLY HAPPENING?

As the yeasts feed on starches in the flour, they produce carbon dioxide, which becomes trapped in the developing gluten network. At the same time lactic acid bacteria (LAB) are busy converting the sugars present in the flour into acetic and lactic acid, which develop flavour in the dough, and as the dough becomes more acidic, gluten bonds tighten and the dough becomes stronger.

HOW TO TELL WHEN YOUR BREAD HAS FINISHED ITS BULK FERMENTATION

- The dough surface starts to dome and curve away from the sides of the bowl.

- You'll see large, stretchy bubbles within the dough or around the edge of the bowl.

- You'll see numerous small blisters over the entire dough surface.

- Your dough will have increased in size (but doesn't need to double).

Stretch and fold

Stretching and folding the dough strengthens the gluten proteins, equalises dough temperature and traps air. The number of stretch and folds is dictated by the strength of gluten development, but it's usually three or four at 30-minute intervals during the early stages of the bulk fermentation phase.

1. With your dough in the bowl, wet your fingers, then take hold of the dough (at 12 o'clock) and stretch it gently upwards into the air as far as possible without tearing it.

2. At full stretch, perform a quick jiggle (sending waves back through the stretched dough), before folding it back downwards into the centre of the bowl.

3. Turn the bowl anti-clockwise so you're now at 3 o'clock, then repeat the stretching and folding action from the top of the bowl as before.

4. Continue folding on all sides (four in total), then flip the dough over so it's domed side up with the folds underneath.

Shaping the dough

Tensioning the surface of the dough helps it hold its form while proving and baking and the boule and batard are great starting points for a huge variety of shapes. If you've made enough dough for more than one loaf, you may need to divide your dough before shaping. You can do this by eye or, for greater accuracy, by weight using scales.

Boule

1. *Pre-shape:* Lightly flour your counter. Turn the dough out of the bowl so that the smooth, domed-shaped top is in contact with the floured counter. Follow the same method (see above) to gently stretch and fold the dough from all sides, then turn the ball of dough over so that it is domed side up again. Cover with an upturned bowl or tea towel to maintain its temperature and prevent it from drying out.

2. While the dough is resting, prepare your round banneton.

PREPARE THE BANNETON

Hold your banneton in one hand and gently sift flour over the sides and base with the other, tilting it as you go. If you've used too much, brush off any excess before the loaf is baked. No banneton? Use a medium-sized bowl lined with a well-floured tea towel.

3. *Final shape:* Let the dough rest for 20 minutes, then flour the domed top of the dough and turn it over using your scraper. Gently stretch and fold the dough again from all sides, then turn it back over so that it's domed side up again.

4. *Tension the dough:* Remove any excess flour from your counter and position the dough at arm's length. Drag the dough ball towards you with both hands, applying downwards pressure on the lower back edge **(1)**. You should see the top surface of the dough become smooth and tight. Take the dough back to the starting position, turning it 180 degrees before repeating this tensioning step. Repeat this step two more times, rotating the dough each time, until you achieve a smooth, tight ball.

5. Lift the dough into the prepared banneton by picking it up with a scraper and supporting the domed side with your other hand. In mid-air, turn the dough over and place it domed side down gently in the banneton. You'll need to remove your supporting hand at the last minute!

Batard

1. *Pre-shape:* Repeat step 1 for shaping the boule (see page 113).

2. While the dough is resting, prepare a long-/oval-shaped banneton (see page 113).

3. *Final shape:* Let the dough rest for 20 minutes, then flour the domed top of the dough and turn it over using your scraper. Gently tease the dough into an elongated egg shape, then take hold of the edge closest to your body, stretch it slightly towards you and fold it into the centre of the oval.

4. Using both hands, take the two side edges and stretch them gently outwards before folding them back into the centre, overlapping each edge slightly. With both hands again, take hold of the top edge of the dough and lift it upwards while folding it back towards your body so that it meets the edge closest to you. Press lightly to seal. Starting at the top of the dough, take sections from the outside edges and overlap them in a stitching method, gently pressing to seal the joins.

5. Finally, with elbows out and using both hands, slide your fingers underneath the top edge of the dough, palms up and thumbs on top, and tightly roll up the dough towards you, removing your thumbs as you go until you meet the edge closest to you. Close the seam by pushing the dough away from you, slightly pushing against the counter using both thumbs, then drag it back towards you with your fingers. Repeat this push/pull step a couple more times until you've created a tight, smooth log shape.

6. Lift the dough into the prepared banneton by picking it up with a scraper and supporting the domed side with your other hand. In mid-air, turn the dough over and place it domed side down gently in the banneton. You'll need to remove your supporting hand at the last minute!

The final prove

To a large extent your recipe dictates the conditions for your final prove.

Yeasted breads
Doughs made with baker's yeast tend to ferment faster, so they're best proved ambient the same day you make the dough. Depending on the temperature and recipe, this could take between 1–3 hours.

Sourdough breads
Sourdough, or dough made with a preferment (and low levels of yeast), is usually cold proved in the fridge overnight. Yeast fermentation slows down, but bacteria continue to feed, developing complex flavours in the dough. An overnight prove followed by an early morning bake will give you the pleasure of a freshly baked loaf on your breakfast table!

YOUR DOUGH IS READY TO BAKE WHEN:

- It has increased in size (it doesn't need to double).

- It looks puffy and jiggly (if it's ambient proved).

- The indentation from a gentle press with your fingertip will slowly fill out again. If the indentation remains, your dough could be overproved. If the indentation bounces back straight away, the dough needs to prove a little longer.

Scoring your loaf

Scoring your loaf enables controlled expansion of the loaf in the early stages of the bake. A loaf that isn't scored will still expand but may burst uncontrollably, often ruining the shape of your loaf. Your loaf is scored on the top to a depth of approx. 5mm. Brush off any excess flour, then score your loaf quickly and decisively. As you get more experienced, experiment with holding the blade at an angle to create the much sought-after lift on your crust, referred to as an 'ear'.

Baking your loaf

Baking tray method
Use this technique if your loaf is too large or too long to fit in the Dutch oven.

1. Preheat your oven with a heavy steel baking tray on the middle shelf and a smaller, deep roasting tin in the bottom. Cut a piece of baking parchment slightly larger than your loaf and place on a wooden chopping board – this is your peel. When you're ready to bake, place your loaf on the parchment, remove any excess flour, then score your loaf using a bread lame or sharp knife (see above).

2. Turn off the oven fan if possible, then slide your loaf (complete with parchment) onto the hot tray. If you're using a tin, place it gently onto the tray. Throw some water into the tray at the bottom of the oven and use a clean plant mister to create plenty of steam around the loaf. After 25 minutes, open the door briefly to release steam and continue to bake your loaf for another 10–15 minutes until the internal temperature is 97°C and a dark golden crust has formed. Allow to cool on a wire rack before cutting the loaf open.

Dutch oven method

For baking hearth loaves (loaves proved in a banneton) or small tins, I prefer the Dutch oven method because it traps the steam around your loaf at the start of the bake, enabling it to expand fully before forming a crust and giving consistently good results. It's how I bake all my loaves at home.

1. Use a large cast-iron or ceramic pan with a lid. If you're baking a lot of bread, you might want to have a dedicated pan as it will get blackened from being subjected to regular high heat in your oven.

2. Place the Dutch oven in your oven while it's preheating (if you're using a tin, check that it will fit).

3. Prepare a parchment paper sling (see page 19) to lift your loaf into the deep pan without risk of burning your hands. When your oven is super-hot, carefully lift the Dutch oven onto a heatproof surface and remove the lid (oven gloves!). Turn your loaf out of the banneton onto the sling, brush off any excess flour, then score your loaf using a bread lame or sharp knife (see opposite).

4. Lift your loaf carefully into the Dutch oven, replace the lid and put in the oven. After 25 minutes, remove the lid and turn your oven temperature down slightly if your recipe contains butter or sweet ingredients, such as dried fruit or honey. Continue to bake your loaf for another 10–15 minutes until a dark golden crust has formed and the internal temperature is 97°C. Remove from the pan and allow to cool before cutting the loaf open.

Oat and honey soda bread

Difficulty: ⌂
Loaf weight: 900g

Prep: 20 mins
Bake: 35–40 mins

Equipment:
  450g loaf tin

200g self-raising flour
120g plain wholemeal
  flour
150g jumbo oats
1 tbsp bicarbonate of
  soda, sifted
1½ tsp fine sea salt
1 tbsp honey
1 tbsp treacle
350g buttermilk

Quick and easy to make, soda bread can be on the table within an hour. To leaven this bread, we use bicarbonate of soda rather than yeast, which gives a distinctive taste and texture and makes it the perfect introduction to the pleasures of real bread. If you're struggling to find buttermilk, add a tablespoon of lemon juice to full-fat milk. Stir and allow to curdle slightly for 30 minutes.

Delicious with salty butter and a bowl of home-made soup or with scrambled eggs and smoked salmon. This loaf will stale quickly, so enjoy it fresh on the day it's made or toast the next day. We get our buttermilk from our local raw milk supplier, Fen Farm Dairy, a by-product of their delicious Baron Bigod brie.

Preheat the oven to 210°C/190°C fan/gas 6–7 and grease your tin thoroughly.

Weigh the two flours, 120g of the oats, the bicarbonate of soda and salt into a large bowl and whisk to combine.

In a jug, measure your honey, treacle and buttermilk and stir to combine. Add the liquid to the flour mix and, using a scraper or a wooden spoon, stir briefly to combine until no dry matter remains. This is more like mixing a cake batter than bread – don't overmix the dough.

Pour the wet mix into the prepared tin and smooth the top with a wet finger. Sprinkle the remaining 30g of oats onto the wet surface. Bake for 35–40 minutes until golden brown and the core temperature is 97°C.

Pain de campagne

Difficulty: ◻ ◻
Loaf weight: 700g

Prep: 5 mins to mix
the preferment,
45 mins active time
Prove: 4–5 hrs
Bake: 35 mins

Day before (preferment)
20g strong white
bread flour
40g dark rye flour
Pinch of active
dried yeast
Pinch of fine sea salt
45g cold water

Bake day
320g strong white
bread flour
40g dark rye flour
½ tsp active
dried yeast
230g water
1 tsp fine sea salt

Adding rye flour to both the preferment and final dough gives this rustic loaf a delicious depth of flavour. We buy our flour from Marriage's, a family-owned local mill just down the road in Chelmsford. We've been working with the team since the bakery opened and I've been lucky enough to visit their amazing mill on several occasions. This bread is perfect for serving with cheese and/or cured meats and enjoying with a glass of red in the summer sunshine.

The night before, mix the ingredients together for the preferment (see page 109). Cover and leave at room temperature.

The next day, weigh the flours into a large bowl. Dissolve the yeast in the water (see page 108 for calculating your water temperature) along with 105g of the preferment and add to the flours. Mix briefly, then cover and rest the dough for 30 minutes.

After resting, add the salt and knead the dough (see page 109) for approx. 5 minutes to achieve moderate gluten development (see the windowpane test on page 110), then place in an oiled bowl to bulk ferment (see page 112). Perform two stretch and folds (see page 113) within the first hour, then either place your dough in the fridge, uncovered, to shape and bake the next day or leave to prove in the bowl for another hour (2 hours total) if you want to bake your loaf today. Maintain your dough temperature at 26°C.

When the dough is ready for its shape and final prove, it should be puffy and increased in size. Follow the instructions on page 114 for pre-shaping a batard, rest the dough for 20 minutes, then final shape into a floured banneton. Prove for 1–2 more hours ambient, checking the dough regularly for signs that it's ready to bake (see page 115).

If you kept your dough in the fridge overnight, let it warm up for an hour in the bowl, then gently pre-shape and final shape in a banneton as above.

Half an hour before your loaf looks ready to bake, preheat the oven and your Dutch oven to 240°C/220°C fan/gas 9.

When your loaf is ready, gently turn it out of the banneton, score (see page 116) and place in the Dutch oven (see page 117). Bake for 25 minutes with the lid on, then remove the lid and bake for another 10 minutes until the temperature is 97°C internally and the loaf is golden brown.

Pain de campagne with confit garlic and oregano

Difficulty: ⏲ ⏲
Loaf weight: 700g

Prep: 5 mins to mix
the preferment,
45 mins active time
+ 1 hr for the garlic
Prove: 4–5 hrs
Bake: 35 mins

1 garlic bulb
300ml olive oil
1 x Pain de Campagne
  final dough (see
  page 121)
1 tbsp dried orgegano
  or small bunch of
  fresh, roughly chopped

NOTE

Next time you have your
oven on, use the heat to
confit a few garlic bulbs
until they're a deeply
caramelised, sweet and
sticky garlic jam. Freeze
until you're ready to
use. Add any leftover
garlic to cooked pasta
with roughly chopped
sundried tomatoes and
olives. Top with a drizzle
of tasty olive oil, black
pepper and a handful
of hard, salty cheese.

Serve slices of this flavoursome bread with a chunky winter soup and a wedge of cheese.

Preheat the oven to 170°C/150°C fan/gas 3.

Take your whole garlic bulb and slice off the top third to expose the inside of each clove. Place cut side down in the oil in a narrow heatproof dish. Cover with foil or a lid and bake for 1 hour – your garlic should still be submerged under the oil with a soft and sticky texture. Give it a little longer if it's not quite there, topping up the oil level as required.

Allow to cool and squeeze each garlic clove out of its pod. Combine with the leftover olive oil and store in the fridge for up to 1 week or place in the freezer.

Make the Pain de Campagne as on page 121. After the first stretch and fold, place the garlic, garlicky oil and oregano onto the surface of the dough and fold into the dough during the second fold. Prove, shape and bake as on page 121.

Focaccia with olives, rosemary and sea salt

Difficulty: ⬚ ⬚
Makes: 500g tray

**Prep: 5 mins to mix
   the preferment,
   45 mins active time**
Prove: 3½–4½ hrs
Bake: 30 mins

Day before (preferment)
50g strong white
   bread flour
10g rye flour
Pinch of active
   dried yeast
Pinch of fine sea salt
40g cold water

Bake day
270g strong white
   bread flour
5g fine sea salt
230g water
5g active dried yeast
50g extra virgin olive oil
Flaky sea salt
Fresh rosemary tips
Pitted black olives

This super-hydrated dough is full of bubbles and is light and airy. Gently press these simple ingredients over the surface for an easy accompaniment to a family-style meal.

The night before, mix the ingredients together for the preferment (see page 109). Cover and leave at room temperature.

The next day, weigh the flour and salt into a bowl. Weigh the water (see page 108 for calculating your water temperature), holding back 30g. Add the preferment and the yeast to the main water, stirring to dissolve.

Add the liquid to the flour and use a dough scraper to fold and chop the dough until no dry flour lumps remain. Trickle half the olive oil down the inside of the bowl and under the dough, encouraging the dough to lift from the bottom of the bowl and 'float'. Cover and rest the dough for 30 minutes, maintaining the dough temperature at 26°C.

After 30 minutes, stretch and fold the dough (see page 113) in the bowl for a minute until it feels strong, then gradually add the reserved water – squeezing and folding it into the dough until incorporated. Allow the dough to rest for 30 minutes, then use the remaining oil to coat a shallow tray large enough to hold the dough and tip the dough onto it.

With oiled/wetted hands, use the stretch and fold technique to strengthen the dough. Turn the dough, taking hold of each side of the dough and folding it into the centre.

Place the dough back into the oiled bowl and continue to bulk ferment (see page 112) for another 1½ hours. Maintain the dough temperature at 26°C and stretch and fold the dough every 30 minutes (twice more).

At the end of the bulk fermentation, pour the dough onto a rimmed baking tray or into a tin lined with baking parchment. The size will dictate the thickness of your baked focaccia.

continued overleaf

Wet or oil your hands and dimple the dough firmly all over with braced fingertips, pressing it out to the corners of the tray/tin. This will take several attempts as the gluten will resist, so allow the dough to relax for a couple of minutes before stretching again.

When the dough has filled the tray/tin, sprinkle with flaky sea salt and push the rosemary tips and pitted olives into it. Leave the dough to prove for 1–2 hours until bubbly on top and risen.

Preheat the oven to 240°C/220°C fan/gas 9, placing a heavy baking tray on the middle shelf and a small deep roasting tin in the bottom of the oven (see page 116).

Bake for 15 minutes, creating some steam if possible by turning off the oven fan and throwing some water into the tin at the bottom of the oven. After 15 minutes, release the steam and bake for another 15 minutes until golden brown.

Focaccia with tomato, prosciutto, mozzarella and salsa verde

Prepare your dough as above. When the dough has relaxed and filled the baking tray/tin, spread quality crushed tinned plum tomatoes all over the dough, dimpling and pressing with braced fingertips. Sprinkle with flaky sea salt and allow the dough to finish proving until bubbly and slightly risen.

Bake as above, then cool. You may need to cover the tomato topping with baking parchment towards the end of the bake to prevent it burning. Arrange 12 slices of prosciutto on the cooled tomato bread, add 250g torn buffalo mozzarella, Salsa Verde (see page 171) and a drizzle of tasty olive oil. Season with flaky sea salt and black pepper.

100% spelt loaf

Difficulty: ▢ ▢
Loaf weight: 840g

Prep: 5 mins to mix
  the preferment,
  45 mins active time
Prove: 4–5 hrs
  (or 2½ hrs, then
  overnight cold prove)
Bake: 35 mins

Day before (preferment and seed soaker)
35g white spelt flour
35g water
Pinch of active
  dried yeast
Pinch of fine sea salt
30g linseed
30g sunflower seeds
10g sesame seeds
70g boiling water

Bake day
190g wholemeal
  spelt flour
190g white spelt flour
230g water
7g active dried yeast
1 tsp honey
12g fine sea salt
Extra seeds for the top
  (optional)

BAKER'S TIP

Soak the seeds the day before to allow them to swell. If dry seeds are added to the dough they 'rob' the dough of water, making it tight and dry.

Nutty, sweet spelt is available as both a white and wholemeal flour. The proteins in spelt behave differently to wheat as they have a higher gliadin to glutenin ratio. This makes spelt a good choice for the gluten intolerant but also means it has more extensibility (the ability to stretch) but less elasticity (the ability to stretch, then return to the same shape), which can make it susceptible to overmixing and gluten breakdown (though this is unlikely to happen if you're hand mixing).

The night before, mix the ingredients together for the preferment (see page 109) and combine the seeds and boiling water to make a seed soaker. Leave both at room temperature, covered.

The next day, weigh the flours into a large bowl. Weigh the water (using the temperature calculations on page 108) and dissolve 70g of the preferment and the yeast in the water with the honey. Add to the bowl. Mix briefly until there is no dry flour, then cover and rest for 30 minutes.

After the rest, add the salt and knead the dough (see page 109) for approx. 5 minutes to moderate gluten development (see the windowpane test on page 110), then place into an oiled bowl with 70g of the seeds spread over the surface of the dough to bulk ferment (see page 112) for 2 hours. Perform two stretch and folds (see page 113) within the first hour (this will incorporate the seeds), then either place your dough in the fridge, covered, to shape and bake the next day or leave to prove in the bowl for another hour to complete the bake today, maintaining your dough temperature at 26°C. Check regularly for the key indicators that your dough has completed the bulk fermentation stage (see page 112).

Follow the instructions on page 113 for pre-shaping a boule, then rest the dough for 20 minutes before completing the final shape. Roll the shaped loaf over a damp tea towel and into a tray of seeds if adding to the top, then place into a floured banneton. Prove for 1–2 more hours ambient, checking regularly. If you kept your dough in the fridge overnight, let it warm up for an hour, then gently shape before a final prove as above.

Half an hour before your loaf looks ready to bake, preheat the oven and your Dutch oven to 240°C/220°C fan/gas 9.

When your loaf is ready, turn it out of the banneton, score (see page 116) and place in the Dutch oven (see page 117). Bake for 25 minutes with the lid on, then remove the lid and bake for another 10 minutes until the temperature is 97°C internally and the loaf is golden brown.

Betsy bread (pain de mie)

Difficulty: ☐☐
Loaf weight: 600g

Prep: 30 mins
active time
Prove: 2½–3½ hrs
Bake: 30–40 mins

Equipment:
450g loaf tin

Roux
110g strong white
bread flour
110g hot milk (65°C)

Final dough
110g milk, plus extra
for brushing
1 tsp active dried yeast
25g honey
240g strong white
bread flour
1 tsp fine sea salt
15g cold unsalted butter,
cut into small pieces

> **NOTE**
>
> The roux can be made
> the day before and stored
> in the fridge but bring it
> to room temperature
> before using.

When I first started experimenting with sourdough my youngest daughter, Betsy, was still living at home. I would make her this loaf, the antithesis of a weighty sourdough, as both treat and respite! The roux method gives a gloriously tender crumb by binding extra liquid into the dough. Delicious warm and spread with butter and jam, perfect for sandwiches or toasted and topped with pâté and a sprinkle of flaky sea salt.

To make the roux, combine the flour and hot milk in a pan and use a fork or whisk to beat and prevent lumps as it thickens. Cover with baking parchment or cling film to stop a skin forming. Cool to room temperature.

Place 220g of the cooled roux in a bowl and chop roughly with your scraper. Warm the milk to the correct temperature (using the calculations on page 108) and add the yeast and honey. Whisk until dissolved, then add to the roux. Weigh the flour into the bowl and mix, using a dough scraper to fold and chop until no dry flour remains. Rest, covered, for 30 minutes.

Turn the dough out onto the counter and add the salt. Knead for about 5 minutes (see page 109) to develop a moderate gluten structure (see the windowpane test on page 110). Sprinkle the butter on the dough, then knead until smooth and strong with no visible butter. Place in a lightly oiled bowl and cover. Find a warm place to maintain the dough temperature at 26°C. Bulk ferment (see page 112) the dough for 1 hour with two folds after 15 and 30 minutes. Prepare a 450g loaf tin by lightly greasing the sides and base – pay particular attention to the corners. Divide the dough in two.

Lightly flour the counter and the surface of each piece of dough and roll the first piece to a 7cm x 15cm length with the long edge next to your body. Fold the length into overlapping thirds, known as a single fold, then turn the dough by 90 degrees and roll out again to 7cm x 15cm. Starting with the short edge next to your body, roll the dough up into a tight log shape. Repeat with the other piece of dough. Place the two rolls into the tin so that the sides of each touch the long sides of the tin, with the tail of each facing the same direction. You will have two mini loaves next to each other. Cover with a cloth and prove for 1–2 hours until almost doubled in size (see page 115).

Preheat your oven to 210°C/190°C fan/gas 6–7.

When the loaf is ready, brush with milk and bake for 30–40 minutes, dropping the oven to 200°C/180°C fan/gas 6 after 10 minutes. Bake until golden and the temperature is 97°C internally. Cover with a cloth so the crust stays soft, then after 10 minutes remove from the tin. Cool on a rack.

Sourdough

Simply put, this is bread raised using a wild yeast culture. There's nothing new or trendy about sourdough. Before baker's yeast was developed at the turn of the century, it was the only way to leaven bread! A growing interest in baking from scratch, accelerated by necessity and home-based work during Covid lockdowns, has seen a rise in the appreciation of this method of making bread. Health benefits aside, the combined effects of carbon dioxide, lactic acid and acetic acid create a deliciously chewy loaf with a robust open crumb and a complex sour flavour.

The thrill of harnessing Mother Nature to create a loaf of freshly baked bread can't be beaten. Sourdough bread keeps so well because its acidity protects the loaf against decomposing microorganisms and the effects of staling, so it's worth making a couple of loaves each time you bake. It also freezes perfectly – great for popping a slice in the toaster.

To make sourdough you'll need to keep a sourdough culture (also known as a 'starter', 'mother', 'chef' or 'leaven'). If you happen to know anyone that keeps a sourdough culture or a friendly baker, then this is your best option to get started as it removes a lot of uncertainty from your baking. We give away sourdough culture to our bake school students so they can continue to feed it at home. We also sell it in dehydrated form in our shops and on our websites.

Although it pains me to say it – creating a sourdough culture from scratch is really a last resort. While it's very satisfying to unleash the life trapped within a grain, it's also a journey fraught with 'what-ifs' and no definitive answers. If you've no option but to start from scratch, turn to page 261.

I'm hoping you're reading this at least ten days before you want to bake, but if your culture isn't ready for action and you're desperate for a bready fix, turn to page 121 and get started with a recipe for some delicious yeasted bread while you nurture your wild yeasts.

Your schedule for success

The jargon

MAINTENANCE

Maintain your culture at 100g and keep it in the fridge when you're not using it. When ready to bake, remove from the fridge and feed for a couple of days beforehand to re-activate. The longer it's been in the fridge unfed, the more days it will need to be fully re-activated. Every time you feed it, discard 90g (90%) and feed the remaining 10g (10%) with 45g of flour and 45g of water. Your culture likes to be warm, so a tall, narrow container with a lid is best. If you're using a Kilner jar or screw top, don't fully clamp it down – your culture will expand and produce fermentation gases!

USING YOUR FRIDGE

The wild yeasts and bacteria in your culture are *very* temperature sensitive. In the chill of the fridge, they're essentially hibernating and can stay this way for weeks, months or even years. As the culture gradually runs out of food, it'll start to look a little different. You'll see alcohol floating on the surface, mould and changes to the colour. The consistency will be very runny and there will be a strong smell of acetone. These signs mean your culture needs feeding before you try to make bread with it – but it's definitely not dead!

FEED

The yeast and bacteria in your culture need food to become active, ready to raise your loaf. Flour, mixed with water, offers them starches and sugars in a readily available form. Any flour will do, though wholegrain flours contain more active enzymes, and your culture will respond more quickly. Your culture can be converted from wheat to rye to spelt just by the flours you feed it with.

DISCARD

Once you've taken your culture out of the fridge and you're feeding it every day to re-activate it, you'll need to 'discard' or it'll get bigger in volume and the food-to-yeast ratio will become diluted. Discard with every feed – the remaining portion of active culture 'inoculates' the fresh flour and water and starts the feeding and multiplying cycle again. If you keep your culture at 100g maintenance, your discard should be very little. I keep mine in a lidded container in my fridge and add to it every time I discard and feed my culture. Eventually, I have enough to make some sourdough crispbreads or crackers (see page 155) or I add the fermented flour to pancake and crumpet mixes.

BUILD

The night before baking, you'll need to 'build' your culture if your recipe requires more than 90g of culture.

Preparing your sourdough culture for a bake

	(AM) DISCARD, FEED, MAINTAIN	(PM) DISCARD, FEED, MAINTAIN
DAY 1	Remove your culture from the fridge and discard 90g. Mix the remaining 10g with 45g of flour and 45g of water. Use a rubber band to show your starting level, then leave somewhere warm for 12 hours. You should see an increase in volume after this time – if there isn't, move your bake schedule back by a day to allow more time for your culture to re-activate.	Discard 90g and mix the remaining 10g with 45g of flour and 45g of water. Use your rubber band to show your starting level. Leave the culture somewhere warm for 12 hours.

	(AM) DISCARD, FEED, MAINTAIN	(PM) DISCARD, FEED, BUILD
DAY 2	Discard 90g and mix the remaining 10g with 45g of flour and 45g of water. Use your rubber band to show your starting level. Leave the culture ambient (19–21°C) for 12 hours.	Refer to your recipe to see how much culture you require, then add at least 10g to that amount for maintaining your culture. Discard the appropriate amount (see example overleaf) and feed the remainder with flour and water. You will now have enough culture for your recipe plus a little extra. Mark the level using a rubber band and leave the culture somewhere warm for 12 hours to double in size.

	YOUR CULTURE IS READY TO USE WHEN:	MAKE YOUR DOUGH USING MOST OF THE CULTURE
DAY 3	• It's doubled in volume but hasn't started to slide back to where it started (see page 261). • When you pull back the surface with a spoon you see lots of bubbles underneath. • The smell is slightly sweet and lactic with an acetic undernote. • It no longer tastes of flour and has a yoghurt-like sour tang.	When you've finished making your dough, add 45g of flour and 45g of water to the 10g of culture that was left over. Place in a clean jar and allow the yeasts to start feeding for an hour or so, then pop into the fridge until the next time you're thinking about baking bread.

EXAMPLE

Your recipe needs 150g, your maintenance feed the day before made 100g and you need to reserve at least 10g to maintain your culture. Total to build is therefore 160g:

1. From your 100g, discard 84g (leaving 16g behind). The 16g represents 10% of the total amount you need for your recipe, plus your 10g extra.

2. Add 72g of flour and 72g of water to the 16g of culture and you'll have 160g.

3. Use 150g in your recipe and feed the remaining 10g with 45g of flour and 45g of water. Your culture is now back to a maintenance weight of 100g.

BULK FERMENTATION EXAMPLE SCHEDULE

12pm–12.30pm	MIX, THEN REST
12.30pm	ADD SOURDOUGH CULTURE (IF APPROPRIATE) AND SALT
12.30–12.40pm	KNEAD TO MODERATE GLUTEN DEVELOPMENT
12.40pm	BULK FERMENTATION BEGINS (2–4 HOURS)
1:10pm	STRETCH AND FOLD 1 (approx. 30 minutes)
1.10pm	FOLD IN INCLUSIONS AT THIS POINT
1.40pm	STRETCH AND FOLD 2 (approx. 30 minutes)
2.10pm	STRETCH AND FOLD 3 (approx. 30 minutes)
2.40pm	STRETCH AND FOLD 4 (if required)
3.40–4.40pm	ANTICIPATED END OF BULK FERMENTATION

Sourdough warning signs and what to do

WARNING SIGNS	WHAT IT MEANS	WHAT TO DO
Culture not doubling in size in 12 hours	Your culture is not active enough to make bread yet	• Keep it somewhere warmer • Continue the feeding schedule for another day
Lots of tiny bubbles on the surface of the culture (see page 261)	Your culture needs a feed	Discard 90% and feed your culture
Culture looks milky and liquid	Your culture needs a feed	Discard 90% and feed your culture
There's a 'snail trail' of culture receding down the sides of the container from where it doubled in size	Your culture has run out of food and has passed its peak	If it's just starting, use your culture in your recipe – it's like it's having a feed! If it has been like that for some hours, give it another feed before using
Dough doesn't look bubbly and full of life	It could be that your culture wasn't active enough or that your dough is too cold	• Make sure your culture is doubling in size before you use it • Maintain your dough at 26°C
Dough feels dry and scratchy and is tough to fold and shape. The baked loaf has a tight crumbly structure	Your flour is very thirsty and there's not enough water in your recipe	Add some more water in small increments and keep a note of how much extra you've added
Dough feels too wet and is difficult to manage	Your flour cannot absorb the amount of liquid in your recipe	Hold back 10% of the water when you first mix the dough. Add the remainder if required. Make a note of how much you kept back
My loaf is flat when I turn it out of the banneton	Your loaf is probably over-proved. The yeasts have consumed so much starch that the dough gluten structure has started to break down	Reduce your bulk fermentation time slightly and keep a close eye on the dough temperature

Classic Magpie sourdough

Difficulty: ❑ ❑ ❑
Loaf weight: 900g

Prep: autolyse 30 mins,
   3½–4½ hrs ambient
   prove
Prove: overnight
Bake: 35 mins

**Day before
(sourdough build)**
100g active sourdough
   culture (see page 133)
68g strong wholemeal
   bread flour
68g water

Bake day
400g strong white
   bread flour
70g strong wholemeal
   bread flour
310g water
10g fine sea salt

This base recipe can be followed for all the sourdoughs that follow. An adaptation of our signature loaf, it is a great starting point for your sourdough baking adventure. It's big and bold with a tangy taste and open crumb. The strong white flour ensures good gluten development with a small amount of wholemeal flour adding flavour and texture. I've kept the hydration relatively low, so you'll be able to practise your stretch and folds and shaping moves without too much stress. When you're feeling more confident or working with thirsty flours, add a little more water, but remember to make a note of how much you added.

The recipe calls for an 'active' sourdough culture. Make sure yours is doubling in size overnight before attempting this recipe. Follow the feeding schedule on page 133 so you're ready to hit the ground running!

Day before: Discard 85g of culture and feed the 15g left with the flour and water. You'll have plenty for the recipe and extra to maintain your culture.

Autolyse (see page 109): Weigh your flours into a bowl. Calculate your water temperature (see page 108), then add 90% to the flour. Hold back 10%. This will help dissolve the salt and is a good opportunity to warm or cool your dough. Use a chopping/scooping/scraping movement with the curved side of your flexible scraper to bring the dough together until no dry parts remain. If necessary, complete using a squeezing action with your dominant hand. Keep the other hand clean – you might need to answer the phone! Cover your bowl and rest the dough for 30 minutes. Maintain the temperature at 26°C. Where you place your dough is going to differ depending on how warm/cool your house is. Use this time to write a fermentation schedule (see page 134), even just on the back of an envelope.

Kneading the dough (see page 109): After 30 minutes, add 110g of the sourdough culture, the salt and remaining 10% of water to the bowl. Use both your scraper (chopping and scooping) and your hand (squeezing) to incorporate, then turn your dough onto the unfloured counter and knead until smooth, strong and elastic with moderate gluten development (see the windowpane test on page 110). This will take approx. 5–8 minutes.

Bulk fermentation (see page 112): Lightly grease your mixing bowl, then shape your dough into a ball. Place back into the greased bowl, cover and begin the bulk fermentation. Maintain your dough temperature at 26°C.

continued overleaf

Stretch and fold (see page 113): After 30 minutes check the dough temperature and complete the first stretch and fold. Cover the bowl and leave for another 30 minutes. Repeat this two more times. After three folds, your dough should feel strong – you can check using the windowpane test (see page 110). Add in another fold if necessary. Continue the bulk fermentation for another 1–2 hours without folding – maintain the dough temperature around 26°C. Your dough has finished its bulk fermentation when the surface starts to dome slightly and curves away from the sides of the bowl, you can see large, stretchy bubbles in the dough and small blisters on the surface and your dough feels jiggly and bouncy.

Pre-shape (see page 113): Pre-shape the dough into a boule. Handle the dough firmly but gently, trying not to deflate too much. Rest for 20 minutes so the gluten can relax.

Final shape: After 20 minutes, use your scraper to lift the dough and gently turn it over, smooth side down, onto a lightly floured surface. Repeat the steps to create a boule, finishing smooth side up. Tighten the boule by removing excess flour from the counter (so the dough sticks slightly) and push down on the outside edges of the ball as you drag the boule in a rounding motion with the outside edge of your hands. Success feels like a tight 'skin' on the outside of the dough. Using a scraper, lift your dough off the counter. Supporting it with your other hand, turn it upside down (sticky side up) into a prepared banneton (see page 113), then place, uncovered, in the fridge.

Overnight cold prove (retarding): Place your banneton in the fridge, uncovered, to retard the dough. If you're worried about fridge smells, let it cool for 30 minutes, then cover. It can stay there for up to 48 hours until you're ready to bake your loaf. Your loaf can be baked straight from cold.

Baking (see page 116): Preheat the oven to 240°C/220°C fan/gas 9 for 30 minutes. Follow the instructions for scoring and baking your loaf in a Dutch oven on pages 116–117. Bake for 25 minutes with the lid on, then remove the lid and bake for another 10 minutes until golden brown and the temperature is 97°C internally.

BAKER'S TIP

To remove any sticky dough, dip your hands into a bag/bowl of white wheat flour, shake loosely to remove the excess, then rub your hands together in a wringing motion over your dough. Most of the dough stuck on your hands will rub off and can be re-incorporated into your mix.

Suffolk wild

Difficulty: ⬜⬜⬜
Loaf weight: 970g

Prep: autolyse 2–3 hrs,
  3½ hrs ambient prove
Prove: overnight
Bake: 35 mins

**Day before
(sourdough build)**
30g active sourdough
  culture (see page 133)
35g Hodmedod's YQ
  or locally grown and
  milled wholemeal
  bread flour
35g stoneground
  white bread flour
50g water

Bake day
220g Hodmedod's YQ
  or locally grown and
  milled wholemeal
  bread flour
140g stoneground
  white bread flour
280g water
20g honey
10g fine sea salt

The selective breeding of grain varieties, coupled with intensive growing conditions and the heavy handling of farm machinery, has created a wheat monoculture. This is not only damaging to our natural environment, but also means that pests and diseases require blanket treatment and climate challenges could potentially wipe out an entire crop. Hodmedod's, an independent Suffolk business just down the road from us, are part of a growing movement to develop more genetically diverse crops of wheat – referred to as YQ (yield and quality). By planting many different 'populations' of wheat in the same field, different strains naturally modify and adapt to local growing conditions, creating a more resilient and diverse crop. We're keen to support this work and proud to use their flour in our bakes.

Wheat grown and milled locally offers a more sustainable approach to breadmaking. It won't necessarily be an easy journey as variability in grain and milling requires a more flexible approach. I suggest you make this by hand and use this recipe as a guide, responding to the needs of the dough. Your water quantities, kneading and fermentation times may need adjusting and your 'wild' may take a few attempts to tame – remember it's all part of your journey as a baker.

The day before, feed your sourdough culture (see page 133).

The next day, combine the flours and 90% of the water (use the temperature calculations on page 108). Hold back 10% of the water required until the kneading stage so that you can assess the absorbency of your flour. Cover and leave to autolyse (see page 137) in a warm place for 2–3 hours.

After the autolyse, add 150g of the sourdough culture, the honey and salt, then complete the mix/knead (see page 137), adding the remaining water if the dough feels stiff and dry. Knead firmly until you have moderate gluten development (see the windowpane test on page 110), then place the dough in an oiled bowl.

Cover the dough and start the bulk fermentation (see page 137). The dough will need to be kept warm (around 26°C) for approx. 3 hours, with a fold every 15 minutes for the first hour and a half (six folds total). After the bulk fermentation is complete, turn your dough out onto the counter. Gently de-gas the dough, shape into a boule (see page 138) and rest for 20 minutes, covered. Gently complete the final shape and place in a prepared banneton.

Follow the Classic Magpie Sourdough instructions (see page 138) for overnight retarding and baking.

East Coast rye

Difficulty: ▢ ▢ ▢
Loaf weight: 700g

....

Prep: autolyse 30 mins,
   3½ hrs ambient prove
Prove: overnight
Bake: 35 mins

....

**Day before
(sourdough build)**
10g active sourdough
   culture (see page 133)
45g light rye flour
45g water

Bread spice mix
20g caraway seeds
10g anise seeds
10g fennel seeds
5g coriander seeds

Bake day
295g strong white
   bread flour
50g light rye flour
25g dark rye flour
260g water
8g fine sea salt

NOTE

Rye flour contains more
active enzymes than
wheat, so reduce the bulk
fermentation by half an
hour if your dough looks
very puffy, particularly
on a warm day.

This hearty, country-style loaf shows off the distinctive texture and taste of rye grain. The dough feels sticky at the start but avoid the temptation to add flour. Hold your nerve and give the wheat flour a little time to develop its gluten network and 'prop up' the rye flour.

You'll see the term 'bread spice' regularly in rye bread recipes, giving each loaf a distinctive flavour. The choice of spices used varies geographically and culturally. Recognisable flavour combinations can be attributed to different regions. Nordic bakers favour dill, fennel, anise and orange zest, whereas Eastern European bakers opt for caraway, coriander, cumin and nigella. If you're not keen on any of the spices in this version, tweak it to create your own blend.

The day before, feed your sourdough culture (see page 133).

Mix together the spices for the bread spice mix. You will have extra for next time. Store in an airtight jar.

The next day, combine the flours and 90% of the water (use the temperature calculations on page 108). Hold back 10% of the water required until the kneading stage so that you can assess the absorbency of your flour. Cover and leave to autolyse (see page 137) in a warm place for 30 minutes.

After the autolyse, add 55g of the sourdough culture, the salt, 10g of the bread spice mix and any water that was held back. Knead the dough until you have moderate gluten development (see the windowpane test on page 110), then place the dough in an oiled bowl.

Cover the dough and start the bulk fermentation (see page 137). The dough will need to be kept warm (around 26°C) for approx. 3 hours with a fold every 30 minutes for the first hour and a half (three folds total). After the bulk fermentation is complete, turn your dough out onto the counter. Gently de-gas the dough, shape into a boule (see page 138) and rest for 20 minutes, covered. Very gently complete the final shape and place into a prepared banneton.

Follow the Classic Magpie Sourdough instructions (see page 138) for overnight retarding and baking.

Torte de seigle

Difficulty: ⬭ ⬭ ⬭
Loaf weight: 800g

·····················

Prep: 15 mins
Prove: 4–5 hrs ambient
Bake: 55 mins

·····················

**Day before
(sourdough build)**
30g active sourdough
    culture (see page 133)
100g light rye flour
100g water (at 30°C)

Bake day
320g dark rye flour
240g water (at 70°C)
10g fine sea salt
White rice flour,
    for dusting
Light rye flour,
    for dusting
Ice cubes, to create
    extra steam

This 'cake of rye' makes a spectacular centrepiece. White rice flour for coating the ball of dough gives a dramatic contrast between the cracked, deeply cratered surface and the dark, tangy interior. Allow the loaf to mature for at least 24 hours before slicing thinly.

The day before, feed the sourdough culture (see page 133). Keep in a warm place overnight.

Prepare somewhere warm for your proving loaf to go – this could be your oven with the light on, a warm bathroom or a high shelf. Measure the flour into a large bowl and pour on your hot water **(1)**. Combine using a squeezing action with your hands **(2)** – the dough will feel very stiff – and leave for 5 minutes, during which time the hot water will dramatically warm up the flour. Add 230g of the sourdough culture and the salt and mix well with a scraper until evenly combined. Cover the dough and bulk ferment (see page 137) in a warm place for 3 hours – no folds are necessary.

Prepare a small round banneton by generously dusting with an equal mix of white rice and light rye flours (or line a bowl with a clean tea towel and dust generously with the same mix). Half-fill a bowl large enough to take your loaf with the same flour mix. Place a jug of water and scraper close by.

At the end of the bulk fermentation your dough should feel puffy and slightly expanded. Wet your scraper in the water and scoop the dough together into one lump. Using wet hands, mould your dough into a ball, pushing any untidy bits to the base of the loaf with wet fingers. Dip the dough ball into the bowl of flour and coat well. Place into the banneton with the well-floured base on the bottom.

Prove the dough for 1–2 hours at 26°C – it will increase in size slightly and the visible flour should start to crack. Preheat the oven to 240°C/220°C fan/gas 9 for 30 minutes with a Dutch oven inside. Cut some baking parchment to a size suitable to support your loaf as you lift it into the Dutch oven.

When you're ready to bake, turn your loaf out of the banneton onto the paper, then rest for 5 minutes. When the surface looks crazed and cracked, lift it into the hot Dutch oven with a couple of ice cubes pushed down the outside of the paper for extra steam. Bake for 25 minutes with the lid on, then take the lid off and bake for 30 minutes until the loaf is a deep brown. Check the internal temperature is 97°C or above before cooling on a rack. Properly stored in a storage bag or bread box, rye bread will last for at least 4–5 days at normal room temperature. Serve thinly sliced.

New potato, spring onion and dill sourdough

Difficulty: ▢ ▢ ▢
Loaf weight: 900g

....

Prep: autolyse 30 mins,
   3½ hrs ambient prove
Prove: overnight
Bake: 35 mins

....

**Day before
(sourdough build)**

10g active sourdough
   culture (see page 133)
20g strong wholemeal
   bread flour
25g strong white
   bread flour
45g water

Bake day

290g strong white
   bread flour
50g strong wholemeal
   bread flour
280g water
120g new potatoes
20g olive oil
½ tsp flaky sea salt
½ tsp black pepper
Bunch of spring onions
Big bunch of fresh dill
1 tsp nigella seeds
10g fine sea salt
Dill fronds or spring
   onions, for garnish

Dill and potato are a classic Scandinavian combination, uniting the freshness and colour of springtime flavours. Make sure you save some dill fronds to decorate the crust of this loaf. Use a waxy potato that will stay firm when roasted and go big on the dill and spring onion.

The day before, feed your sourdough culture (see page 133).

The next day, combine the flours and 90% of the water (use the calculations on page 108). Hold back 10% of the water required until the kneading stage so that you can assess the absorbency of your flour. Cover and leave to autolyse (see page 137) in a warm place for 30 minutes.

Preheat your oven to 200°C/180°C fan/gas 6. Chop your potatoes into 3cm chunks, leaving the skins on. Place in a shallow roasting tray with the olive oil and salt and black pepper. Roast for 20–30 minutes until lightly coloured and soft enough to pierce with a knife. Chop the spring onions into 5mm rings, retaining as much green as possible. Remove the woody stalks from the dill and roughly chop. Once the potatoes have cooled, add the spring onion, dill and nigella seeds and mix to combine.

After the autolyse, add 80g of the sourdough culture, the salt and any water that was held back. Knead the dough until you have moderate gluten development (see the windowpane test on page 110), then place the dough in an oiled bowl and spread the cooled potato mix on top of the dough. This will be incorporated during the first stretch and fold and continue to be spread evenly through the dough with each subsequent stretch and fold.

Cover the dough and start the bulk fermentation (see page 137). The dough will need to be kept warm (around 26°C) for approx. 3 hours with a fold every 30 minutes for the first hour and a half (three folds total). After the bulk fermentation is complete, turn your dough out onto the counter. Gently de-gas the dough, shape into a boule (see page 138) and rest for 20 minutes, covered. Prepare your banneton by flouring as usual, then lay some large dill fronds or spring onions in the base. Very gently complete the final shape and place your loaf on top, smooth side down.

Follow the Classic Magpie Sourdough instructions (see page 138) for overnight retarding and baking.

Chorizo, cheese and chilli sourdough

Difficulty: ⬜⬜⬜
Loaf weight: 800g

....

Prep: autolyse 30 mins,
    3½ hrs ambient prove
Prove: overnight
Bake: 35 mins

....

**Day before
(sourdough build)**

10g active sourdough
    culture (see page 133)
20g strong wholemeal
    bread flour
25g strong white
    bread flour
45g water

Bake day

50g strong wholemeal
    bread flour
250g strong white
    bread flour
230g water
60g red onion
1 tbsp olive oil
70g chorizo sausage
    (precooked weight)
70g smoked Cheddar
    cheese, cut into
    1cm cubes
5g ground sweet
    paprika
30g Jalapeño Pickles
    (see page 243),
    drained
6g fine sea salt

We love developing new recipes. They're usually the result of much discussion and experimentation, though I must confess when first introduced to this one I wasn't sure about the idea of adding cooked chorizo to dough, though on reflection the principle is no different from meaty pizza! I can confirm it tastes delicious, so big thanks to our head baker, Guy Watts, for this curveball.

If you're making your own pickles, prepare them at least 1 day before. The day before baking, feed your sourdough culture (see page 133).

The next day, combine the flours and 90% of the water (use the temperature calculations on page 108). Hold back 10% of the water required until the kneading stage so that you can assess the absorbency of your flour. Cover and leave to autolyse (see page 137) in a warm place for 30 minutes.

Preheat your oven to 190°C/170°C fan/gas 5. Chop your onion into 1cm dice and toss in the olive oil. Place on a baking tray and roast for 20 minutes until soft and beginning to caramelise. Chop the chorizo into 1cm dice, place on a separate baking tray and roast for 20 minutes until the oils flow and the sausage is lightly crisped. Cool the onion and chorizo, then add to the diced cheese, paprika and jalapeño pickles. Incorporate any oil from the chorizo.

After the autolyse, add 60g of the sourdough culture, the salt and any water that was held back. Knead the dough until you have moderate gluten development (see the windowpane test on page 110), then place the dough in an oiled bowl and spread the chorizo cheese mix on top of the dough. This will be incorporated during the first stretch and fold and continue to be spread evenly through the dough with each subsequent stretch and fold.

Cover the dough and start the bulk fermentation (see page 137). The dough will need to be kept warm (around 26°C) for approx. 3 hours with a fold every 30 minutes for the first hour and a half (three folds total). After the bulk fermentation is complete, turn your dough out onto the counter. Gently de-gas the dough, shape into a boule (see page 138) and rest for 20 minutes, covered. Very gently complete the final shape and place into a prepared banneton.

Follow the Classic Magpie Sourdough instructions (see page 138) for overnight retarding and baking.

Malted double chocolate sourdough

Difficulty: ⬭ ⬭ ⬭
Loaf weight: 700g

Prep: autolyse 30 mins,
4½ hrs ambient prove
Prove: overnight
Bake: 35 mins

**Day before
(sourdough build)**
10g active sourdough
culture (see page 133)
45g strong white
bread flour
45g water

Bake day
290g strong white
bread flour
25g cocoa powder
15g red malt flour
25g malt extract
220g water
5g fine sea salt
20g dark chocolate
bake-stable chips
50g dark chocolate bar,
roughly chopped
into chunks
30g white rice flour
(optional)

Flavoured with malt extract, malt flour and heavily studded with two types of chocolate, we just can't get enough of this! Serve it toasted with salty butter and marmalade for the ultimate breakfast treat. The choc chips are 'bake stable' as they hold their form and re-solidify when cool, whereas the chopped chocolate will stay slightly soft and stud the loaf with irregular streaks and chunks. Buy the best-quality chocolate you can afford with a high percentage of cocoa solids.

The day before, feed your sourdough culture (see page 133).

The next day, weigh the flour, cocoa powder and malt flour into a large bowl and mix well to combine. Dissolve the malt extract in 90% of the water (using the temperature calculations on page 108). Hold back 10% of the water required until the kneading stage so that you can assess the absorbency of your flour. Cover and leave to autolyse (see page 137) in a warm place for 30 minutes.

After the autolyse, add 70g of the sourdough culture, the salt and any water that was held back. Knead the dough until you have moderate gluten development (see the windowpane test on page 110), then place the dough in an oiled bowl and spread the two types of chocolate on top of the dough. The chocolate will be incorporated during the first stretch and fold and continue to be spread evenly through the dough with each subsequent stretch and fold.

Cover the dough and start the bulk fermentation (see page 137). The dough will need to be kept warm (around 26°C) for approx. 4 hours with a fold every 30 minutes for the first hour and a half (three folds total). The sweetness of this dough will make bulk fermentation slower, so although you'll be following the same Classic Magpie Sourdough instructions, allow at least another hour (4 in total) in the bowl after the stretch and folds.

After the bulk fermentation is complete, turn your dough out on the counter. Gently de-gas the dough, shape into a boule (see page 138) and rest for 20 minutes, covered. While not essential, if you have white rice flour to dust your banneton it will give a nice contrast to the dark colour of the loaf. Very gently complete the final shape and place into the prepared banneton.

Follow the Classic Magpie Sourdough instructions (see page 138) for overnight retarding and baking.

Fig and fennel sourdough

Difficulty: ⏏ ⏏ ⏏
Loaf weight: 800g

....

**Prep: autolyse 30 mins,
  3½ hrs ambient prove**
Prove: overnight
Bake: 35 mins

....

**Day before
(sourdough build)**
10g active sourdough
  culture (see page 133)
20g strong wholemeal
  bread flour
25g strong white
  bread flour
45g water

Fig and orange soaker
70g dried figs, chopped
  into 1cm dice
10g fennel seeds,
  toasted
20g orange juice
5g orange zest

Bake day
300g strong white
  bread flour
60g strong wholemeal
  bread flour
270g water (at 30°C)
7g fine sea salt
Fennel flower/leaf,
  for garnish (optional)

This has been on our bread menu since the beginning and its devotees protest vociferously if we ever give it a little rest or tweak the formula. Spread it with marmalade for breakfast and toast it for cheese at lunch. It even makes great crispbreads if sliced thinly and dried out in the oven.

The day before, feed your sourdough culture (see page 133) and combine all the ingredients for the fig and orange soaker.

The next day, combine the flours and 90% of the warm water. Hold back 10% of the water required until the kneading stage so that you can assess the absorbency of your flour. Cover and leave to autolyse (see page 137) in a warm place for 30 minutes.

After the autolyse, add 85g of the sourdough culture, the salt and any water that was held back. Knead the dough until you have moderate gluten development (see the windowpane test on page 110), then place the dough in an oiled bowl and spread the fig and orange soaker on top of the dough. This will be incorporated during the first stretch and fold and continue to be spread evenly through the dough with each subsequent stretch and fold.

Cover the dough and start the bulk fermentation (see page 137). The dough will need to be kept warm (around 26°C) for approx. 3 hours with a fold every 30 minutes for the first hour and a half (three folds total). After the bulk fermentation is complete, turn your dough out onto the counter. Gently de-gas the dough, shape into a boule (see page 138) and rest for 20 minutes, covered. Prepare your banneton by flouring as usual, then lay a fennel flower or some leafy fronds in the base. Very gently complete the final shape and place your loaf on top, smooth side down.

Follow the Classic Magpie Sourdough instructions (see page 138) for overnight retarding and baking.

Prune and pink peppercorn sourdough crispbreads

Difficulty: ⌀
**Makes: 12 medium
or 6 extra-large
crispbreads**

Prep: 30 mins
Chill: 12–16 hrs
Bake: 25–35 mins

Day before
1 tsp pink peppercorns
40g soft dried prunes
5g flaky sea salt
160g wholemeal
   rye flour
100g strong white
   bread flour
130g wheat or rye
   sourdough culture
   (you can use active
   or stored discard)
   (see page 132)
120g cold water

These Scandinavian-style crispbreads were traditionally stored suspended on wooden poles – hence the hole in the middle. Mini versions make gorgeous gifts with ribbon threaded through the holes. Recently I've been making these crispbreads dinner-plate size and serving as a shared platter to start a meal. Heaped with herring, thinly sliced cheese, cured meats and dotted with pickles and herbs, they're a real conversation piece! Leave the prunes and peppercorns out if you prefer them plain. Either feed your sourdough starter to make enough for the recipe or use some discarded starter.

On a chopping board, use the side of a sharp kitchen knife to crush and flatten the peppercorns. Chop or blend the prunes into a paste with the sea salt and combine with the peppercorns – it's important there are no pieces larger than 1mm otherwise you won't be able to thinly roll your crackers.

Combine the prune paste with all the remaining ingredients in a bowl and mix until no dry bits remain. The dough will be quite stiff but will soften slightly as the sourdough ferments. Cover and refrigerate for 12–16 hours.

The next day, line a couple of baking sheets with baking parchment and preheat your oven to 200°C/180°C fan/gas 6.

Divide the dough into 12 pieces (or 6 for large sharing crackers) and shape into balls. Use wholemeal rye flour to dust your counter. Keep turning the dough as you roll to create a disc approx. 1–2mm thick. Cut out the centre of each using a small round cutter or a metal screw-cap bottle top.

Lay each circle onto a lined baking sheet (they can be quite close as they won't spread) and use a pastry docker or the tines of a fork to press deep holes into each crispbread. Traditionally this is done with a knobbled rolling pin called a Kruskavel. This not only looks decorative but helps the dough dry out while baking.

Bake for approx. 10 minutes, then turn over to bake for 5–10 minutes until lightly browned. Slide off the sheets (and paper) onto the metal racks of the oven. Turn the temperature down to 120°C/100°C fan/gas ½ and bake for another 10–15 minutes. Make sure they are all fully crisped, then leave in the (turned off) oven with the door left slightly ajar until completely cool. Once cool, store in an airtight container. These keep well for a few weeks.

Pizza

Birthday parties, film nights, teenage sleepovers or just hanging out with friends – some of the many reasons why pizza holds a special place in all our hearts. A visit to the New York pizzeria Roberta's a year after opening was the initial inspiration for our pizza. We wanted bold flavours, a thin and crispy base and a generous crust so our customers could enjoy the unique flavour of our long-fermented sourdough.

One night shortly after the US trip, an Italian baker called David knocked on the door and asked for a job. His passion for bread and pizza was infectious and so our techniques and flavours shifted back across the Atlantic. David also taught me to 'throw the dough' – something that never fails to wow. This is his recipe for the perfect pizza:

1/ Respect your ingredients – choose quality over quantity.

2/ Take your time – don't rush your dough.

3/ Make it with love (you know it makes sense).

You can learn a lot about someone by watching them make pizza. There's the thinly stretched and 'less is more approach', with just a whisper of carefully selected ingredients – they want to be sure the base stays crisp and each flavour shines through. Then there's the kitchen sink approach – weighed down with sauce and piled high with charcuterie, vegetables and cheese – sagging as it's transported to the lips, trailing stringy mozzarella and a potential mudslide of toppings. What's so wonderful about pizza is that they're both going to taste great! Pizza is eminently customisable, relatively inexpensive, simple and quick.

To say we use our bakery space intensively would be an understatement. Through the night, the bakers spread themselves into all sections, leaving a fine coating of flour on every surface. In the early morning, before the pastry team arrive, they wipe and sweep, removing all evidence of their occupation. As the bakers say their goodbyes, the pastry team move swiftly to occupy their mix bench and shaping tables then, finally, as the pastry team are phoning in their next-day orders, the chefs stake the final claim for their prep and larder re-stock. Six days a week, the bakery then falls silent, save for the whirr and clunk of fans and compressors.

But not on a Saturday. It's pizza night. Today the bakery doesn't rest.

The phone is ringing off the hook with orders as soon as we open and from 5 pm lights are dimmed and tables are laid. The temperature of the oven is pushed to its limit, orders are organised with military precision, dough is shaped and topped, and there's an unsteady stack of pizza boxes in the corner. Over the course of a couple of hours, hundreds of pizzas are pulled from the oven to be finished with tasty oils, fresh leaves and dressings before being packed into boxes and heading out of the door.

Sourdough pizza dough

Difficulty: ▢ ▢

Makes: 4 x 250g pizzas (for hungry people)

....

Prep: 30 mins, 3 hrs ambient prove with stretch and folds

Prove: overnight

....

Day before (sourdough build)

20g active sourdough culture (see page 133)

90g strong white bread flour

90g water

Bake day

500g strong white bread flour

290g water

20g olive oil

10g salt

Fine semolina, for sprinkling

For a flavoursome Saturday night pizza, you'll need to start reactivating your culture on Wednesday if it's kept in the fridge, so forward planning is required here. The pizza dough will keep, wrapped, in your fridge for a couple of days and freezes well – though make sure you use it within a month.

Remove your sourdough culture from the fridge a few days before making this dough. Leave it ambient and complete maintenance feeds (see page 133) for at least 2 days to re-energise your culture. You'll be building your culture from 100g to 200g the night before making your pizza dough, then once your dough is made, it'll need to ferment overnight,

The next day, in a large bowl combine the flour and water (see page 108 for calculating your water temperature) to incorporate all the dry matter and create a shaggy dough. Rest the dough in a warm place for 30 minutes.

Add 180g of the sourdough culture, the oil and salt.

Complete the mix by kneading the dough on your counter for 3–5 minutes following the instructions on page 109, during which time the oil will be absorbed into the dough. Perform three stretch and folds (see page 113) 30 minutes apart for the first 1½ hours, then prove the dough for another hour before dividing and shaping into four mini boules (balls) (see page 113).

Toss the balls in flour and place, well-spaced out, in a shallow lidded container in the fridge to ferment overnight. The next day, use your scraper to separate them if they have batched together.

Shaping your pizza

THE LEDGE

Remove your dough from the fridge 30 minutes before you're ready for shaping.
Preheat your oven and prepare your equipment (see opposite). Take your first ball of
dough and toss it in some flour, making sure it's well coated and won't stick to your
fingers. Press gently on the counter to flatten and de-gas it, then, with your fingertip,
trace a circle about 1cm in from the edge of the dough. This will mark the crust or
cornicione as it's known in Italy (literal translation 'ledge').

Place the fingertips of both hands (fingers together, poised like a meerkat) about 1cm
below the top edge of the traced circle and press firmly as you move back towards your
body – stopping when you're about 1cm from the bottom of the circle. Press firmly
enough to feel the counter through your fingertips – you need to boss the dough! If your
hands are quite large, tuck your little fingers in so they don't compress the edge of the
circle (your crust). Give the dough a quarter turn and repeat the pressing action until
you've compressed all the central area evenly and only the outer crust remains puffy.

STAGE 1: THE STEERING WHEEL

With both hands, pick up the dough at the top edge, just inside the crust, between your
fingers and thumbs. Move your hands along the edge, turning the dough like a steering
wheel as the weight of the dough causes it to stretch. The speed you need to turn your
wheel of dough is dictated by the rate of stretch. When the gluten in the dough is fully
relaxed, it stretches easily, but as you work the dough it will start to tighten and shrink
back. If you find this happening, just let the dough relax on a floured surface for a
couple of minutes before resuming. This method of stretching your dough works fine –
let it have some relaxation time between your stretches and you can achieve a large circle
of dough. But if you want to show off your pizza moves (and who doesn't!) read on . . .

STAGE 2: THE BRIDGE

Make both hands into a fist, then place both knuckles together with your thumbs facing
you at chest height. This is your bridge. Using the shaping method from Stage 1, achieve
a circle of approximately 18cm, then place the circle on top of your 'bridge'. The sides
and crust should be draping over your hands. Gently separate your fists outwards
towards the edges of the dough to stretch it, taking care to not overstretch the middle.
Keep shuffling the dough around on your fists so each stretch is from a different direction
to achieve a circle the size and thinness you like.

THE THROW

From here, if you're up for it, it's a neat segue into throwing your pizza – push your
arms upwards and throw the dough into the air while rotating your wrists anticlockwise
to spin the dough. You need height but also centrifugal force to stretch the dough outwards.
Be brave – practice makes perfect and it's a great party trick once you've nailed it!

Baking your pizza

HOME OVEN

Perfect pizza in a kitchen oven requires lots of bottom heat, a high temperature and a short bake. Preheat your oven to its maximum temperature with heavy baking trays or pizza stones on the shelves. Don't be tempted to bake more than two pizzas at a time – it just gets too steamy. Cut a piece of baking parchment the size of each pizza. When the oven is really hot, place your pizza base onto the paper. Top, then use the paper to slide the pizza onto a chopping board (or the back of a cold baking tray) – this is your peel. Open the oven and quickly slide the pizza (and paper) onto the hot tray or pizza stone. Bake for 7–10 minutes depending on the ferocity of your oven until bubbly and crisp.

WOOD-FIRED PIZZA OVEN

Whether traditional, space age or your DIY pride-and-joy, a wood-fired oven gives a delicious smoky flavour to your pizza. Dough comes alive in such intense heat – huge bubbles push against the surface while smaller blisters create a leopard-spotted crust. The size of your oven interior will dictate the weight of dough needed for each pizza – in my small Ooni I scale each dough ball at 170g. Light your oven in plenty of time – it needs to be at least 300°C. Sprinkle semolina on your wooden peel, laying your dough on it before topping. Gently slide your pizza into the oven, checking it regularly over the next few minutes and rotating with a circular metal peel until cooked to perfection. Depending on your oven this could vary from 1 to 5 minutes.

Margherita

Difficulty: ⬭
Makes: 4 pizzas

Prep: 20 mins
Bake: 1–10 mins
depending on oven

4 x Pizza Bases
(see page 160)
300g tinned tomatoes
Bunch of fresh basil
300g fior di latte
mozzarella, grated
or cubed
Flaky sea salt

Basil oil
Generous bunch of
fresh basil
300ml extra virgin
olive oil

NOTE

If you're making more
than one pizza in a
wood-fired oven outside,
use your domestic oven
to keep your cooked
pizzas warm until you're
ready to eat.

Years ago, I attended a study day at the School of Artisan Food in Nottinghamshire. For lunch we were served the longest pizza I've ever seen – it stretched the width of their deck oven and was presented on a wooden plank down the centre of the table. Truly magnificent. The beautifully buckled and blistered crust was simply topped with tomato, mozzarella cheese and fresh basil. It's the simplest things in life that are often the best!

Preheat your oven (see page 163).

Strip the leaves from a generous bunch of basil and place in the jug of a small blender. Add the oil and blitz until puréed. Allow to sit for 10 minutes, then strain through a sieve, pressing the basil with the back of a spoon, then discard. Store it in the fridge for up to a month, bringing to room temperature before you use it.

Prepare your pizza sauce by simply crushing the tomatoes in your hands directly over your dough or using a stick blender to blend the contents briefly – just a couple of quick blasts or your sauce will become too wet. Spread in the centre of your dough using the back of a ladle. Avoid the crust and go easy with your tomato sauce – the water content can result in unappetising puddles and a soggy bottom.

Lay basil leaves onto the sauce like the petals of a flower so you're sure of getting one per slice. Laying the basil under the cheese protects the delicate leaves from the searing oven heat while infusing the sauce underneath. Sprinkle on your cheese, using less in the middle and more towards the edge. Don't worry if some cheese lands on the crust – you'll have added crispy bits.

Bake your pizza (see page 163) until bubbling and golden brown. Sprinkle with fresh basil leaves, some of the basil oil, flaky sea salt and a generous grind of black pepper.

Firestarter

Difficulty: ⏻
Makes: 4 pizzas

Prep: 45 mins
Bake: 1–10 mins
  depending on oven

4 x Pizza Bases
  (see page 160)
2 red onions
4 tbsp olive oil
300g tinned tomatoes
2 garlic cloves, finely
  chopped
300g fior di latte
  mozzarella, grated
  or cubed
300g mascarpone
120–150g nduja
Salsa Verde (see
  page 171)
Finely sliced fresh red
  or green chilli

It was midday, early September, in southern Italy. The sun was relentless, a dry wind was blowing ice-cream wrappers along the deserted streets and I had optimistically stopped in this small town in the hope of getting some relief from an insect bite. As I wandered past shuttered shop doors, I noticed some very familiar signs on several buildings around the town. On closer inspection, I realised I had stumbled upon Spilinga, the home of nduja (pronounced 'endooya'), a product we love using at the bakery.

Here, the spicy paste, made from a mix of pork, chilli, herbs and fat, is spooned onto mascarpone, creating cool, creamy, hot and spicy contrasts. It's quite powerful, so go easy until you get the measure of it. Nduja is also great spread on toast with grilled vegetables or warmed over a flame at the table like a fondue, dipping sourdough bread into the melting paste as it forms puddles of spicy oil.

Preheat your oven 200°C/180°C fan/gas 6.

Slice your onions in half from tip to base, then slice again into 5mm-thick semi-circles. Place the semi-circles onto a baking sheet and toss in the olive oil, season with sea salt and black pepper and cover with foil or baking parchment. Roast in the oven for 20–30 minutes until soft but not brown. Remove from the oven and cool.

Turn up your oven to its maximum temperature (see page 163).

Prepare your pizza sauce by simply crushing the tomatoes in your hands directly over your dough or using a stick blender to blend the contents briefly – just a couple of quick blasts or your sauce will become too wet. Spread into the centre of your dough using the back of a ladle. Avoid the crust and go stingy rather than generous – too much sauce will give you a soggy bottom!

Finish assembling your pizza by layering on the chopped garlic, roasted onions and a handful of mozzarella. Finally, use a teaspoon to place dollops of mascarpone on top, aiming for one in each slice, then top each dollop with a little nduja – it's hot, so go easy if you're not actually a Firestarter!

Bake your pizza (see page 163) until bubbling and golden brown. The mascarpone should be gently spreading as the chilli oil pools around it. Drizzle with salsa verde and finish with the chilli – enjoy with a cold beer.

Annie

Difficulty: ⌂
Makes: 4 pizzas

Prep: 15 mins
Bake: 1–10 mins
  depending on oven

4 x Pizza Bases
  (see page 160)
100ml double cream
300g smoked ham
200g fior di latte
  mozzarella, grated
  or cubed
200g Taleggio cheese,
  cut into 2cm cubes
Drizzle of runny honey

Named after the Southwold lifeboat, this has remained one of our most popular pizzas and we make a donation for every one sold. Make sure you use good-quality thickly sliced ham and be generous with the black pepper.

Preheat your oven (see page 163).

Using a large spoon, spread the cream over the centre of the dough, avoiding the crust. Tear the smoked ham into large pieces (don't slice it) and distribute evenly, then add a handful of mozzarella and Taleggio and a generous grind of pepper.

Bake your pizza (see page 163) until bubbling and golden brown. We like to serve it with a grind of black pepper and a drizzle of runny honey. Just don't tell the Italians.

NOTE

Fior di latte, a hard, low-moisture cow's milk cheese, is a magnificently melty mozzarella that blisters and browns without turning oily. It comes in block form or grated. Cube it yourself for big cheesy mouthfuls or grate for even distribution and those crispy edges. We use it as a base layer on all our pizzas. Fresh cow's milk mozzarella is inexpensive and creamy and melts to a satisfying level of stringiness. Buffalo mozzarella, smoother and sweeter than cow's, is a treat best saved for tearing over your cooked pizza. The delicious contrast of cold creamy curds melting into a molten bubbling sauce can't be beaten.

The green man

Difficulty: ▢
Makes: 4 pizzas

Prep: 45 mins
Bake: 1–10 mins
 depending on oven

4 x Pizza Bases
 (see page 160)
2 large red onions
4 tbsp olive oil, plus
 1 tbsp for the courgette
3 medium-sized
 courgettes
1 tsp lemon zest
250g tinned tomatoes
2 garlic cloves,
 finely chopped
300g fior di latte
 mozzarella, grated
 or cubed
100g chilli pearls
100g pitted Kalamata
 olives

Salsa verde
Small bunch of
 fresh mint
Small bunch of fresh
 flat-leaf parsley
50g capers, drained
250ml extra virgin
 olive oil

NOTE

Imagine each bite as you
lay your toppings down,
so the flavours you have
created can be enjoyed
in each mouthful.

Slicing the courgette into ribbons means they collapse quickly in the oven heat as the cut edges char. Use slightly less tomato sauce on this pizza to prevent it becoming soggy. To make this pizza vegan, simply substitute the mozzarella for a vegan version.

Salsa verde literally translates as 'green sauce', so this is a great opportunity to use up some of those herbs lurking in the back of your fridge. If you haven't come across this versatile dressing before, you're in for a treat. It's fresh and punchy – a blend of mint, parsley and capers with plenty of olive oil.

Preheat your oven 200°C/180°C fan/gas 6.

Slice your onions in half from tip to base, then slice again into 5mm-thick semi-circles. Place the semi-circles onto a baking sheet and toss in the olive oil, season with sea salt and black pepper and cover with foil or baking parchment. Roast in the oven for 20–30 minutes until soft but not brown. Remove from the oven and cool.

Turn up your oven to its maximum temperature (see page 163).

Using a vegetable peeler, start at the base of each courgette and peel thin, wide ribbons towards the tip. Work your way around until you're left with a thin seedy core about 1cm thick. Finely chop the core and toss in a bowl with the ribbons, a tablespoon of olive oil and the lemon zest.

Strip the mint leaves from the stalks and place in a blender with the parsley (stalks attached) and drained capers. Add half the olive oil and blitz until chunky. Make sure all the parsley stalks have disappeared. Add the remaining oil to create a loose sauce. This keeps in the fridge for 2 weeks.

Prepare your pizza sauce by simply crushing the tomatoes in your hands directly over your dough or using a stick blender to blend the contents briefly – just a couple of quick blasts or your sauce will become too wet. Spread into the centre of your dough using the back of a ladle. Layer on the courgette ribbons, chopped garlic, roasted onion, mozzarella, spicy chilli pearls and Kalamata olives.

Bake your pizza (see page 163) until bubbling and golden brown, then finish with a generous splash of salsa verde.

La dolce vita

Difficulty: ⬚⬚
Makes: 4 pizzas

Prep: 1½ hrs
Bake: 1–10 mins
   depending on oven

4 x Pizza Bases
  (see page 160)
2 red onions
4 tbsp olive oil
300g tinned tomatoes
2 garlic cloves, finely
  chopped
300g fior di latte
  mozzarella, grated
  or cubed
200g Parmesan cheese,
  grated
Handful of fennel
  fronds, chopped

**Pork and fennel
meatballs**
1 tbsp fennel seeds
400g pork mince
2 large eggs
100g fresh breadcrumbs
  (preferably sourdough)
2 garlic cloves,
  finely chopped
½ tsp chilli flakes
1 tsp flaky sea salt

Braised fennel
3 fennel bulbs
2 tbsp olive oil

Pork and fennel – what a classic. Think fennel-coated salami in an Italian deli or warm porchetta, fragrant with fennel seeds, wedged between slices of focaccia.

   Cook a double batch of meatballs ahead of time and open-freeze, then defrost before use so you're always ready for pizza night. They're also great tossed with pasta and a garlicky tomato sauce.

Preheat your oven to 200°C/180°C fan/gas 6.

To make the meatballs, toast the fennel seeds and grind to a rough powder, then combine with the remaining ingredients. Prepare a lined baking tray. Have a small bowl of water nearby and use wetted hands to scoop walnut-sized pieces of the pork mix, form into balls and place on the tray. Bake for 10 minutes until lightly browned. Cool, then chill or freeze until required.

To make the braised fennel, remove any woody stalks, keeping the delicate fronds to use later. Trim underneath the bulbs to remove dry woody pieces and level the bases. Sit each bulb on its base, then cut straight down to slice it in half. Place the cut side on the chopping board and slice the fennel into 5mm thick sections from tip to base – don't worry if they fall apart. Repeat with the remaining fennel halves. Place into a shallow baking tin, toss in the oil to coat and season well with sea salt and black pepper. Roast, uncovered, for 10 minutes, then add enough water to come up to half the height of the fennel. Cover the dish with foil or a lid and cook for 20 minutes until tender. Cool and remove from any remaining liquid.

Slice your onions in half from tip to base, then slice again into 5mm thick semi-circles. Place onto a baking sheet and toss in the olive oil, season and cover with foil or baking parchment. Roast for 20–30 minutes until soft but not brown. Remove from the oven and cool.

Turn up your oven to its maximum temperature (see page 163).

To assemble the pizza, prepare your pizza sauce by simply crushing the tomatoes in your hands directly over your dough or using a stick blender to blend the contents briefly – just a couple of quick blasts or your sauce will become too wet. Spread into the centre of your dough using the back of a ladle. Layer on the chopped garlic, braised fennel, roasted onion, mozzarella and finally the meatballs.

Bake your pizza (see page 163) until bubbling and golden brown, then finish with Parmesan and chopped fennel fronds.

Love me tender

Difficulty: ⌂
Makes: 4 pizzas

Prep: 30 mins
Bake: 1–10 mins
  depending on oven

4 x Pizza Bases
  (see page 160)
2 bunches of
  long-stem broccoli
Zest of 1 lemon
400g fresh breadcrumbs
  (preferably sourdough)
4 tinned anchovy fillets,
  minced, or miso paste
2 garlic cloves, finely
  chopped
2 tbsp olive oil
150ml double cream
200g mascarpone
300g fior di latte
  mozzarella, grated
  or cubed
Rocket leaves dressed
  with olive oil
Thinly sliced fresh red or
  green chilli
Parmesan shavings

Pangrattato, or poor man's Parmesan, is testament to the ingenuity of the cucina povera style of Italian cooking. Use a rustic-style loaf for chunky breadcrumbs and make extra – these moreish nibbles will disappear very quickly if you've a beer in your hand and a crowd in your kitchen.

Bright green, crunchy long-stem broccoli is available all year round. In late summer you could switch to purple-sprouting broccoli.

Preheat your oven (see page 163).

Place a pan of salted water on the hob and prepare a bowl of iced water. If your broccoli is chunky, remove the woody ends, then slice along the length of the stalks until the stems are 5mm thick. When the water is boiling, add the broccoli and cook for 2–4 minutes (depending on thickness). Drain and run under cold water for a couple of minutes, then place in the ice bath. When the broccoli is completely cold, place it on some kitchen paper to dry, then toss it with the lemon zest, seasoning well.

Combine your breadcrumbs with the minced anchovy (or miso paste), finely chopped garlic, salt, pepper and olive oil, then fry in a frying pan over a medium heat until golden, turning regularly to brown all sides.

Mix the double cream and mascarpone together and season well. Spread over your dough using the back of a ladle and avoiding the crust. Scatter over the mozzarella, then arrange the broccoli stems like the spokes of a wheel. Sprinkle generously with the breadcrumbs, then bake (see page 163) until the cheese is bubbling and golden brown.

Finish with some dressed rocket leaves, red chilli and Parmesan shavings.

Pastries and Enriched Dough

Breads containing sweeteners (sugar, honey, etc) or fats (eggs, milk or butter) are known as enriched. They create a soft, tender dough that is delicious to eat and slow to stale.

It's all about the layers

In my previous life, butter was something that sat softly, in a dish, waiting to be spread on toast or an ingredient to be rubbed into flour or creamed with sugar for a cake, but now handling butter by the kilo has become my new normal. Straight from the fridge, it's hard and rigid, dry (never greasy) and ready to be floured and rolled into thin sheets.

Lamination is the fascinating (time-consuming – good things come to those who wait) process of trapping layers of fat between dough. Starting with one sheet of butter sandwiched between two layers of dough, a series of folds creates multiple layers that increase exponentially until a cross-section looks like pliable geological rock strata. Adding yeast into the equation causes expansion between the butter layers, before finally a hot oven turns the water content of the butter into a puff of steam, caramelising and separating the layers to crumb-shattering proportions.

This chapter starts with an in-depth recipe for that most popular pastry, the croissant. We'll cover the base dough, butter preparation, layering and folding that is common to all the laminated pastries in this section. Once you've mastered the croissant process, this dough becomes a blank canvas as you expand your repertoire by wrapping the rich dough around coffee and chocolate and creating sweet and savoury fillings for swirls and Danish pastries.

We've developed a bit of a reputation for croissants 'as big as your head' (obviously the head in question depends on whether you're a babe in arms or the Incredible Hulk) and yes, I can say with some certainty, ours are undoubtedly on the generous side. Yet while size does matter (wink), the true mark of the perfect pastry is a golden crisp exterior that shatters into hundreds of delicious shards as you bite into it.

Croissants (aka cro-dough)

Difficulty: ⏻ ⏻ ⏻
Makes: 9 full-sized and
  2 mini croissants

Prep: 2–3 day process
  with 1½ hrs active time
Bake: 12–15 mins

Equipment: Straight
  rolling pin (no handle)
  60cm ruler

500g strong white
  bread flour (protein
  level 12–14%)
75g caster sugar
5g fine sea salt
25g cold good-quality
  unsalted butter
7g active dried yeast
140g water (at 20°C)
140g cold full-fat milk
250g cold good-quality
  unsalted butter (for
  Day 2 lamination)
2 x Egg Wash (see
  page 251)

This master dough for croissants is a 2–3 day process. Your dough needs time to rest and develop flavour overnight before it's laminated and shaped, then finally it will need proving and baking. Try to choose a day when the temperature in your kitchen is between 15–21°C. Temperature is critical – too cold and your butter layers could crack and the pastry will be slow to prove. Too warm and the butter layer will become greasy and ooze out and the dough will be puffy with fermenting gas.

Keep practising – your pastries will taste great even if they're a bit wonky while you're learning!

Day 1

Weigh your flour, sugar and salt into a large bowl and combine with the rounded edge of your scraper. Chop your butter into small chunks, then rub into the flour/sugar mix until it resembles fine breadcrumbs. Add the yeast to the warm water, stir to combine, then add your milk. Pour the yeasted liquid over the dry ingredients and combine, using your scraper to scoop around the bowl, then perform a chopping action across the middle of the dough. Repeat these movements until all the dry bits are mixed in and a rough dough has formed.

If you're using a stand mixer, use your dough hook on slow speed to bring the dough together, stopping when there are no more dry bits and a rough dough has formed.

Cover the dough and leave to rest for 20–30 minutes at room temperature. After resting, tip your dough out onto the (unfloured) counter and knead for 3–5 minutes until you have a smooth, extensible dough, using the windowpane test (see page 110) to check for moderate gluten development. Form the dough into a ball and either wrap tightly in greased cling film or use a lidded greased tub (with room for some expansion). Place the dough into the fridge to chill overnight, ready to be laminated the next day.

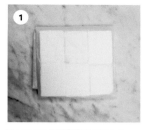

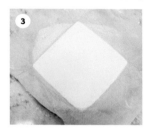

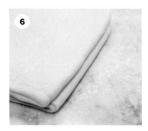

Day 2

Prepare your butter block by dividing the cold butter into six equal slices. Lay the butter in the centre of a large piece of baking parchment, two rows of three, butted up next to each other. Tightly fold the paper over the butter on all sides, like wrapping a present, placing the folds of paper underneath **(1)**. Using the centre of your rolling pin (if you use the tip or edge, it will break the paper), bash and roll the butter into an even square – merging the separate pieces into one smooth, even layer **(2)**. Unwrap then rewrap the butter parcel, allowing it a bit of space to expand so that eventually it is approx. 20cm square. Your butter should still be cold but also slightly bendy. Too cold and it will crack when rolled between the dough layers. If it has become greasy, pop it back in the fridge until it firms up a little. A good test is to extend your butter (while still attached to the paper) over the edge of the counter by 10cm. If it droops slightly, it has the correct pliability – if it stands straight like a board, it's too cold.

Remove the dough from the fridge – it will be a puffed-up, yeasty, sweet-smelling ball. Use your rolling pin to flatten and shape it into a 30cm square. Try not to pull the edges of the dough to form your shape – this will just make the edges thinner – instead, slide your fingers underneath the dough, palms up, and ease the thicker dough from the centre out towards the edges.

With your dough at the correct size, unwrap your butter, leaving it attached to the paper. Using the paper as support, lower the butter in a diamond shape over the dough square **(3)**, then gently peel the paper away from the butter. Fold the edges of the dough over the butter to completely enclose it, pinching the edges tight **(4)**, then turn it over so the seams are underneath.

Folding: Roll the dough parcel out to 60cm long – keeping the width approx. 20cm – then complete your first book fold by folding up the bottom edge about 10cm **(5)** and folding down the top edge to meet it. Now fold the entire length in half horizontally across the middle to create a 'book' of dough **(6)**. Wrap the 'book' in baking parchment or cling film and chill for 30–45 minutes for the gluten to relax. Take care to not leave it too long as the butter will become hard and brittle and may crack when re-rolled.

Remove the dough from the fridge, placing it on a lightly floured counter with the long seam on the right or left side. Roll to 60cm long x 20cm wide and complete a second book fold. Wrap and refrigerate for 30–45 minutes.

continued overleaf

Preparing the dough for croissants: Remove the dough from the fridge for the last time and roll to 52cm long x 22cm wide – it will be approx. 5mm thick. Rolling your dough to this thickness can be a challenge as the dough will be tight after being folded a few times. Go easy with the flour on your counter – too much and your dough will keep sliding and shrinking back. If necessary, take a short rest to allow your dough (and you) to relax. When you've reached the right size, use a knife or pizza cutter to trim 1cm off the rolled edge to create a tidy rectangle approx. 50cm x 20cm (hang on to the trimmings – see pages 222 and 224). Your dough is now fully laminated with many buttery layers – give yourself a pat on the back!

Remembering the adage 'measure twice, cut once', use a knife to mark (not cut) 5 x 10cm spaces along the top edge of the dough. Then from the bottom left-hand edge, mark 5cm followed by 4 x 10cm followed by another 5cm. Join up the lines from the top left down to the 5cm mark on the bottom edge to create your nine full-size croissants and two narrow ones. When you're satisfied you have marked the shapes correctly, cut along the lines cleanly using a knife or pizza cutter.

Shaping: Shaping one at a time, take the base of each triangle in your right hand with your thumb placed across the dough and gently tease out the dough to lengthen it slightly (gently stretching it so it doesn't snap and tear). Lay the base of the triangle on the counter close to your body and create a small roll-over to get the shaping started (about 2cm), then gently tension the dough at the pointed end and start pushing and rolling the croissant away from you using the flat of your hand, continuing to stretch the dough slightly as you move towards the tip of the triangle. You should now have a croissant made up of seven or eight 'wraps' of dough. Place the croissant seam side down (to stop it unravelling as it proves) onto a baking parchment-lined baking tray, leaving a space between each one.

Proving: Brush your egg wash over the pastries and prove in the oven with the light on (an ideal proving cupboard as it creates enough heat to keep the temperature at about 26°C) and a mug of boiling water for humidity. Prove for 1½–2 hours until the pastries are jiggly when you gently shake the tray and the layers are starting to separate. Briefly remove your pastries from the oven while it's preheating to 195°C/175°C fan/gas 5–6, applying a second coat of egg wash very gently to your pastries while you wait.

Baking: Bake for 12–15 minutes, turning the tray after 10 minutes. When they're ready, your croissants will be a glossy, deep golden brown with crisp overlapping layers.

BAKER'S TIP

When butter gets too warm, it's absorbed into the dough and will no longer keep the layers separate. If necessary, pop your dough into the fridge briefly to chill it. Take care though that your butter doesn't harden too much or the cold butter will crack and splinter into shards, causing the layers to become uneven.

Pain au mocha

Difficulty: ☐ ☐ ☐
Makes: 10

....

Prep: 2–3 day process
    with 1½ hrs active time
Bake: 12–15 mins

....

Equipment: Piping bag
    with a 5mm round tip

....

1 x Croissant Dough
    (before lamination)
    (see page 180)
Egg Wash (see
    page 251)

Chocolate dough
10g cocoa powder
20ml strong cold
    brewed coffee

Mocha ganache
120g dark chocolate,
    chopped
40g unsalted butter
40g glucose or
    golden syrup
60g caster sugar
60ml strong brewed
    coffee
60ml double cream

Adding layers of flavoured or coloured dough will certainly raise your pastry game and draw admiring glances. I learnt this beautiful technique from fellow baker David Nizi after spending some time at his Herefordshire bakery. When your pastries are baked and cooled, fill them with rich ganache. Breakfast will never be the same again!

Follow the instructions for making the croissant dough (see page 180), but before wrapping and placing in the fridge overnight, remove 150g of dough.

Weigh the cocoa powder into a small bowl, add the coffee and combine to create a paste. Knead the paste into the 150g of dough until there is no visible streaking. Form the flavoured dough into a flattish rectangle and either wrap tightly in greased cling film or use a lidded greased tub (with room for some expansion of the dough). Refrigerate the doughs overnight.

Prepare the mocha ganache by placing the chocolate into a heatproof bowl with the butter, glucose/syrup and sugar. Heat the coffee and cream in a pan until steaming (but not boiling), then pour over the chocolate. Don't be tempted to stir – just leave it undisturbed for 5 minutes to allow the heat to stay in the bowl, then stir briskly to form a glossy, smooth ganache.

Allow to set at room temperature. The ganache keeps well and can be made the day before – this will allow the chocolate and butter to firm up.

The next day, leave the flavoured dough in the fridge while you laminate and fold the main dough (see page 181). When the dough has rested after the final fold, remove from the fridge and roll out to 40cm x 20cm. Remove the flavoured dough from the fridge and roll this out to 40cm x 20cm too, using flour to stop the delicate dough sticking to the counter **(1)**.

Brush the surface of the main dough very lightly with water **(2)** – it's important that the dough is completely covered (no dry patches) but not soaking wet – just lightly moist.

Place the flavoured dough centrally on the main dough and smooth with your fingers so it covers the whole surface **(3)**. Working from the centre of the dough to the edges, use a rolling pin to apply firm pressure – pushing out all the air bubbles and bonding the surfaces together **(4)**.

Continue to roll the dough until it is 50cm x 30cm, then trim the edges back to 48cm x 28cm. If you get a persistent air bubble, carefully prick it with the point of a sharp knife.

Prepare to cut the dough into ten rectangles by marking a line horizontally across the centre of the dough **(5)**, then marking the top and bottom horizontal edge into five equal sections. Join the marks at the top and bottom of the dough to create four vertical lines. You will now have ten rectangles marked on your dough, approximately 8cm wide x 14cm long.

When you're happy the dough is correctly divided up, cut along the lines cleanly using a sharp knife or pizza cutter. Roll each rectangle so that the chocolate layer is on the outside **(6)** then place the rolled pastries on a baking parchment-lined baking tray seam side down and spaced slightly apart.

Using a small sharp knife, gently score staggered cuts in the top surface of the dough 2cm in length and 2mm deep **(7)** – you will just be able to see the main dough colour through the cut. Carefully egg wash the surface of the pastries, then prove, egg wash again and bake following the croissant method (see page 182).

When the pastries are completely cool, make a hole at each end of all the pastries with a sharp knife, big enough to take the nozzle of a 5mm round piping tip. Fill your piping bag with the ganache – it should be a pipeable consistency – and insert the tip through the hole in each pastry, pushing it through to the centre, then pipe in some ganache as you pull the tip out. Repeat from the other end. In total this will be about 40g of ganache. For quality-control, I would suggest you cut the first one in half across the middle to check you're squeezing hard enough before continuing with the rest!

Pain au chocolat

Difficulty: ❑ ❑ ❑
Makes: 10

Prep: 2–3 day process
with 1½ hrs active time
Bake: 12–15 mins

1 x Croissant Dough
(before lamination)
(see page 180)
2 x 100g bars of
good-quality dark
chocolate
Egg Wash (see
page 251)

As a child I thought Coco Pops was the only acceptable way to get chocolate into the first meal of the day – now I know better! Use the best-quality chocolate you can find and enjoy these while they're still warm!

Follow the instructions for making the croissant dough (see page 180) and place in the fridge overnight.

The next day, roll the dough to the same final size as the Pain au Mocha recipe (see page 185) and follow the same cutting pattern.

Take the bars of dark chocolate and, using a warm knife, cut thick batons about 1cm wide and 8cm long. You will need 20 (2 per pastry).

For each pastry, place your rectangle of dough with the short edge next to you and press a chocolate baton about 1cm in from the short edge. Fold the dough over the chocolate baton, rolling away from you until you can't see it, then add in the second baton before completing the roll.

Place on a baking tray, egg wash and prove. Score the surface of each pastry as before (see page 185), then egg wash and bake following the croissant method (see page 182).

Cinnamon buns

Difficulty: ☐☐☐
Makes: 12

Prep: 2–3 day process
with 1½ hrs active time
Bake: 12–15 mins

Equipment: 10cm
silicone moulds
(optional)

1 x Croissant Dough
(before lamination)
(see page 180)

Cinnamon butter
150g soft unsalted butter
75g caster sugar
60g light brown sugar
20g ground cinnamon
1 tbsp lemon juice

Cinnamon sugar
200g caster sugar
20g ground cinnamon

These delicious pastries are one of our hero products. I've watched as they're unravelled and fed into the mouths of children, hopping like baby birds, sugar crunching underfoot. How do you eat yours? There's always a race to get to the front before we sell out, customers shuffling along the queue, anguished looks and contingency plans being made as the basket on the counter empties, relief flooding over their faces as someone appears in the kitchen doorway bearing another heaped tray.

Follow the instructions for making the croissant dough (see page 180) and refrigerate overnight.

The next day, follow the method for laminating the croissant dough until you have completed both sets of folds and the dough has rested in the fridge (see page 181). While your dough is resting between folds, prepare your cinnamon butter by beating the soft butter with the rest of the ingredients until smooth, but not aerated. Make your cinnamon sugar by combining the sugar and cinnamon.

Roll your dough to 38cm wide x 44cm long. When you've reached the right size, use a knife or pizza cutter to trim about 1cm off the rolled edge to create a tidy rectangle, approximately 36cm x 42cm.

Using a palette knife, spread the cinnamon butter generously over the surface of the dough, leaving a 1cm gap on the edge closest to you. Starting at the short edge furthest away from you, roll the dough tightly in a long log shape until you finish next to your body with the seam sitting underneath the log. Wrap the entire roll carefully in cling film, baking parchment or heavy-duty re-usable plastic and place in the freezer for 30 minutes.

After 30 minutes, remove the log from the freezer and slice into 12 rounds. At the bakery we prove and bake our buns in 10cm diameter silicone moulds. These contain the melting cinnamon butter so it caramelises deliciously on the bottom of the pastry. If you have nothing suitable in your kitchen, lay each round on a baking parchment-lined baking tray with space to expand – they'll still be delicious and you'll have crispy, sugary bits on your tray to snack on.

Prove and bake following the croissant method (see page 182) – best not to egg wash as it helps the sugar stick to the pastry. As soon as you can handle the pastries, toss them in a bowl of cinnamon sugar and enjoy still warm.

Apple and raisin chai swirls

Difficulty: ☺ ☺ ☺
Makes: 12

....

Prep: 2–3 day process
with 2 hrs active time
Bake: 12–15 mins

....

1 x Croissant Dough
  (before lamination)
  (see page 180)
½ recipe Chai Custard
  (see page 254)
Egg Wash (see
  page 251)
Approx. 150g icing sugar

Chai raisins
1 chai teabag
100ml boiling water
200g flame raisins

Roasted apple
5 firm eating apples
½ tsp ground cinnamon
⅛ tsp ground cloves

Take pain au raisin to the next level with a generous filling of spiced custard, apples and raisins and a sprinkle of cinnamon sugar to finish.

Follow the instructions for making the croissant dough (see page 180) and refrigerate overnight.

The next day, follow the method for laminating the croissant dough until you have completed both sets of folds and the dough has rested in the fridge (see page 181).

Prepare your custard and leave to cool before using. To make the chai raisins, add the chai teabag (or some chai spices in a muslin bag) to the boiling water. Add the raisins and leave to infuse.

Preheat the oven to 200°C/180°C fan/gas 6.

Peel, core and cube your apples into 1cm square pieces and toss the apple in the cinnamon and cloves. Roast for 20 minutes, stirring halfway through. Remove and cover with a tray while cooling – this will keep them soft.

Roll your dough to 38cm wide x 44cm long. When you've reached the right size, use a sharp knife or pizza cutter to trim about 1cm off the rolled edge to create a tidy rectangle approximately 36cm x 42cm. Spread the surface of the dough with the chai custard, leaving a gap of 1cm along the edge nearest your body. Gently squeeze any excess liquid from the raisins (keep the leftover spiced liquid to create your icing glaze) before sprinkling them, then the apple cubes, evenly over the surface of the custard.

Starting at the short edge furthest away from you, roll the dough tightly in a long log shape until you finish next to your body with the seam sitting underneath the log. Wrap the entire roll carefully in cling film, baking parchment or heavy-duty re-usable plastic and place in the freezer for 30 minutes.

After 30 minutes, remove the log from the freezer and slice into 12 rounds. Lay each round on a baking parchment-lined baking tray, with space to expand, and egg wash. Prove until jiggly, egg wash again and bake following the croissant method (see page 182).

While your pastries are cooling, mix the icing sugar with a few tablespoons of the chai tea water to form a thickish paste that will fall off the back of a spoon. Drizzle the icing over your pastries.

Bacon, blueberry and maple swirls

Difficulty: ❑❑❑
Makes: 12

Prep: 2–3 day process
with 1½ hrs active time
Bake: 12–15 mins

1 x Croissant Dough
(before lamination)
(see page 180)
100ml maple syrup
60g blueberries
280g streaky bacon
rashers, rind off
100g sesame seeds
Egg Wash (see
page 251)
Flaky sea salt

Bacon crumb
6 streaky bacon
rashers, rind off

Inspired by the popular bacon, blueberry and maple French toast on our menu, this pastry is sweet, sticky, salty and sharp – superb!

Follow the instructions for making the croissant dough (see page 180) and refrigerate overnight.

The next day, follow the method for laminating the croissant dough until you have completed both sets of folds and the dough has rested in the fridge (see page 181).

Roll your dough to 38cm wide x 44cm long. When you've reached the right size, use a sharp knife or pizza cutter to trim about 1cm off the rolled edge to create a tidy rectangle, approximately 36cm x 42cm.

Brush the surface of the dough generously with 3 tablespoons of the maple syrup, then sprinkle with the blueberries, pressing them into the surface slightly. Lay down the bacon rashers vertically, slightly overlapping them so they form a sheet with no gaps.

Starting at the short edge furthest away from you, roll the dough tightly in a long log shape until you finish next to your body with the seam sitting underneath the log. Sprinkle a rimmed baking tray with sesame seeds, then lightly egg wash the outside of the whole roll before rolling in the seeds to coat. Wrap the entire roll carefully in cling film, baking parchment or heavy-duty reusable plastic and place in the freezer for 30 minutes.

Meanwhile, prepare your bacon crumb by baking or grilling your bacon rashers so they are crispy and dried out – take care they don't burn or they will taste bitter. Allow to cool, then crumble into small pieces. After 30 minutes, remove the log from the freezer and slice into 12 rounds. Lay each round on a baking parchment-lined baking tray, with space to expand, and egg wash over the cut surface.

Prove, egg wash again and sprinkle with some flaky sea salt before baking following the croissant method (see page 182).

As soon as the pastries are out of the oven, brush liberally with more maple syrup and sprinkle the crispy bacon pieces over the surface.

Cheesy Marmite twists

Difficulty: ⊓ ⊓ ⊓
Makes: 20

....

Prep: 2–3 day process
with 1½ hrs active time
Bake: 10–12 mins

....

1 x Croissant Dough
(before lamination)
(see page 180)
Egg Wash (see
page 251)

Marmite filling
50g Marmite
150g soft unsalted butter
100g strong Cheddar
cheese, grated

This deeply divisive spread has found its way into quite a few of our products over the years. Choose a strong-flavoured, mature hard cheese and don't listen to the naysayers – they don't know what they're missing! This recipe works equally well with puff pastry – just follow the cutting pattern and method.

Follow the instructions for making the croissant dough (see page 180) and refrigerate overnight.

The next day, follow the method for laminating the croissant dough until you have completed both sets of folds and the dough has rested in the fridge (see page 181). While your dough is resting between folds, prepare your filling by beating the Marmite and butter until smooth but not aerated.

Roll your dough to 35cm x 45cm, with the longer edge next to your body. Use a knife or pizza cutter to trim the edges. This will leave you with a rectangle approximately 33cm x 42cm. Spread the Marmite butter over the lower half of the dough, then sprinkle two-thirds of the cheese on top. Fold the dough sheet in half by lifting the top edge over the cheese and Marmite, so that it meets the bottom edge (closest to your body). Your Marmite/cheese layer will now be sandwiched between two layers of dough. Wrap carefully in cling film, baking parchment or heavy-duty re-usable plastic and freeze for 30 minutes or refrigerate for a couple of hours to firm up.

When it's time to continue, preheat the oven to 195°C/175°C fan/gas 5–6.

Remove the dough from its wrapping and place it with the long-sided open seam next to your body. Score vertically in 2cm increments, then use a knife or pizza cutter to cut cleanly into 20 pieces. Taking each piece separately, arrange the rectangles of dough so that you have the narrow open seam next to your body. Use the knife or cutter to make a vertical cut from the open bottom edge, stopping about 1cm from the top edge so that you've created two 'legs' that are attached at the top.

Working quickly and handling the dough as little as possible to stop it getting too warm, stretch each piece gently, then turn your hands in opposite directions to create a twist. Each twist will be about 25cm. Finish by pinching the open ends to seal, then place onto a baking parchment-lined baking tray with space around to expand and gently egg wash.

Prove the plaits until puffed up and jiggly (see page 182), then egg wash again and sprinkle with the remaining Cheddar. Bake for 10–12 minutes.

Danish pastries

Difficulty: ⬓ ⬓ ⬓
Makes: 12

Prep: 2–3 day process
with 1½ hrs active time
Bake: 12–15 mins

1 x Croissant Dough
(before lamination)
(see page 180)
Egg Wash (see
page 251)

Danish pastries are usually a fast weekend sell-out. Crisp pastry, rich custard, fresh fruit – the perfect excuse for getting in a few of your five-a-day. Our team love playing with colour and flavour combinations as we move through the seasons, so we usually prove and bake our Danish with just their custard filling then, after cooling, we layer on colourful summer berries, spiced autumn fruit, crumbles and nutty textures, fresh herbs and flowers, jams, curds and glazes.

Follow the instructions for making the croissant dough (see page 180) and refrigerate overnight.

The next day, follow the method for laminating the croissant dough until you have completed both sets of folds and the dough has rested in the fridge (see page 181). While your dough is resting between folds, prepare your chosen custard (see following recipes) so it's cooled and ready to use.

Roll your dough to 32cm long x 42cm wide. When you've reached the right size, use a knife or pizza cutter to trim about 1cm off the rolled edge to create a tidy rectangle, approximately 30cm x 40cm. Mark your dough with notches at 10cm intervals along the top and bottom edge and divide the dough horizontally into 3. This should give you 12 squares, each 10cm x 10cm. If you need to make any adjustments to achieve this, use your rolling pin before cutting the dough. When you're happy you have 12 squares, cut your dough with a sharp knife.

Follow the photos opposite to create the 'kite'. We love this shape as it creates a deep central space to fill with fruit and custard without the risk of everything falling off. When you've finished shaping your pastries, brush lightly with egg wash and prove until jiggly and puffed up (see page 182).

When your pastries are ready for baking, use 2 dessertspoons (one to scoop, the other to release) to fill the space in the centre of the pastry with your chosen custard, pushing down slightly in the centre to de-gas the dough. A generous spoonful should be enough – the custard shouldn't rise above the surface of the dough.

Finally, egg wash and bake following the croissant method (see page 182). Allow to cool before filling and decorating with your chosen flavours.

Poached pear, blackberry and bay Danish pastries

Difficulty: ☐ ☐ ☐
Makes: 12

Prep: 2–3 day process with 1½ hrs active time
Bake: 12–15 mins

12 x ready-to-bake
 Danish Pastries
 (see page 196)
Bay Custard
 (see page 255)
Egg Wash (see
 page 251)
225g blackberries
Icing sugar, for dusting

Poached pears
800ml water
200g caster sugar
4 fresh bay leaves, plus
 more for decorating
4 star anise
6 Conference pears

Bay sugar
8 fresh bay leaves
70g caster sugar

I've been obsessively experimenting with bay recently – there's a lot growing in my garden. I like its grassy, spicy taste, often overpowered in soups and rich stews. It's great for infusing custards, poaching liquids for fruit, jams and syrups and for making a bright green sprinkling sugar. Save a few leaves for decoration. Those glossy green leaves peeking out amongst the poached pears and shiny blackberries look amazing – get the camera out!

Make your custard using the base method (see page 254) and following the additions for the bay custard.

Poach the pears a couple of hours before you need them by placing the water, sugar, two of the bay leaves and the star anise in a deep pan. Bring to a very gentle simmer. Peel the pears, leaving them whole and with the stalks intact, then lower into the hot liquid. Cut a circle of baking parchment slightly larger than the diameter of the pan and fold it in half then half again. Cut the tip off the folded paper approximately 1cm in from the pointed end, then unfold the paper (it will now have a hole in the centre for steam to escape) and place over the simmering pears. This 'cartouche' (as it's known), will keep the pears in contact with the gently bubbling poaching liquid. After 20 minutes, test the pears with the tip of a sharp knife. You're looking for a soft, granular texture with a slight resistance – how long it takes to achieve this depends on their ripeness.

To make the bay sugar, rip the spines and woody stems from the bay leaves and place in a spice grinder with the sugar. Blitz until you have a fine pale green sugar. This will keep for several weeks in an airtight jar.

Fill your pastries with the cooled custard. Egg wash and bake following the croissant method (see page 182). Allow to cool slightly before topping.

Lift the pears out of the poaching liquid onto kitchen paper and slice from tip to base, creating a smooth curve as you remove the core. Place the poaching liquid back over the heat along with a couple more bay leaves and reduce by gently simmering until it becomes a thick syrup – it should drip slowly off a spoon. Push three slices of pear into the custard centres, tuck in a couple of blackberries, drizzle over the bay syrup and decorate with glossy green bay leaves and a sprinkle of bay sugar and icing sugar.

Rhubarb and ginger crumble Danish pastries

Difficulty: ☐☐☐
Makes: 12

Prep: 2–3 day process
  with 1½ hrs active time
Bake: 12–15 mins

12 x ready-to-bake
  Danish Pastries
  (see page 196)
Chai Custard
  (see page 254)
Egg Wash (see
  page 251)
Icing sugar, for dusting

Ginger crumble
125g plain flour
25g demerara sugar
25g caster sugar
½ tsp ground ginger
75g unsalted butter

Poached rhubarb
400g rhubarb
Juice of 1 orange
70g caster sugar
100ml water

Delicious though they are, the understated colours of autumnal apples and pears, winter spices and nutty fruitcakes can make our counter displays a little more challenging during the colder months. We get very excited when new season rhubarb is spotted – it's a sign that spring is on its way and our pastries will soon be pretty in pink, shouting 'choose me'! For this version, we use chai custard and finish with a spiced crumble for texture (a gingernut biscuit works fine, too).

Make your custard using the base method (see page 254) and following the additions for the chai custard.

Preheat the oven to 210°C/190°C fan/gas 6–7.

Make the crumble by combining all the ingredients except the butter in a bowl with a pinch of fine sea salt. Melt the butter and drizzle over the dry mix. Stir with a fork to coat the flour and sugar and form irregular clumps.

Spread the crumble mix on a baking tray and bake for 10–15 minutes. Use a spoon to redistribute the crumble after 10 minutes and monitor the colour closely towards the end of the bake time – it burns easily!

To poach the rhubarb, trim the ends and cut into batons on the diagonal, 6cm long and 2cm wide. Thick stalks need to be cut in half from top to tail first. Put in a deep baking dish so that all can sit in the poaching liquid.

Juice the orange and pour into a small pan. Add the sugar and water and bring to the boil, then pour the liquid over the prepared rhubarb and cover the dish with cling film or a lid to retain the heat so that the rhubarb gently poaches. Keep checking and remove the rhubarb from the liquid as soon as it feels soft. Allow to cool on a rack, then store in the fridge.

Make the rhubarb syrup by placing the leftover poaching liquid into a small pan. Reduce by gently simmering until it becomes a thick syrup – it should drip slowly off a spoon.

Fill your pastries with the cooled custard. Egg wash and bake following the croissant method (see page 182). Allow to cool slightly before topping. Assemble the pastries by layering three pieces of rhubarb on the custard and drizzling with rhubarb syrup. Finish by sprinkling over the crumble and a dusting of icing sugar.

Honey, fig and sesame Danish pastries

Difficulty: ☐ ☐ ☐
Makes: 12

Prep: 2–3 day process
   with 1½ hrs active time
Bake: 12–15 mins

12 x ready-to-bake
   Danish Pastries
   (see page 196)
Fig Leaf Custard
   (see page 255)
Sesame Seed Honey
   Brittle (see page 257)
Egg Wash (see
   page 251)
6 fresh ripe figs
Drizzle of honey
Icing sugar, for dusting

I spent a blissful week hanging out in the garden of a house in Italy where the figs were ripening so quickly they were dropping into my lap. On arriving back home, I immediately planted a fig tree in the garden and I'm pleased to say this year it has produced a small crop!

Make your custard using the base method (see page 254) and following the additions for the fig leaf custard.

Prepare your brittle (see page 257, substituting honey for sugar and using sesame seeds). Store the brittle in a cool, dry place until you're ready to use it.

Fill your pastries with the cooled custard. Egg wash and bake following the croissant method (see page 182). Allow to cool slightly before topping.

After baking, prepare your figs by cutting them each into six segments from tip to base. Arrange the fresh figs in the custard, drizzle with honey and go wild with the sesame honey brittle and a sprinkling of icing sugar.

SOME FUN FIG FACTS

- Crushed fig leaves smell like figs taste – isn't that amazing? Try toasting the leaves lightly under a hot grill to bring out their coconut, caramel sweetness.

- Hanging a few fig leaves under the head of your hot shower will make your bathroom smell so delicious!

Brioche dough

Difficulty: 🍞 🍞

Makes: 10 x 50g
doughnuts, 6 x 80g
burger buns or
1 small loaf

Prep: 40 mins
Rest: 6 hrs or overnight

250g strong white
bread flour
25g caster sugar
5g fine sea salt
½ tsp unwaxed
lemon zest
100g eggs (2 eggs),
lightly beaten
35g cold water
7g active dried yeast
60g cold unsalted butter

This buttery dough tastes wonderful in sweet and savoury bakes. We use it for our doughnuts, fruit and custard-filled morning buns and sticky babka loaves, but its subtle sweetness is also perfect as the base for savoury tarts and burger buns.

When you're working with lots of butter, keep things as cool as possible to prevent the dough becoming greasy – chill your ingredients and knead with the heel of your hand, rather than your palm. If you're using a stand mixer, remember it generates heat through friction, so go easy on the mix length, particularly in summer.

Brioche needs a minimum 6 hours in the fridge before shaping and proving (overnight is better) to firm up and develop its unique flavour.

Weigh your flour, sugar, salt and zest into a large bowl and use a plastic scraper to combine. Weigh your lightly beaten eggs and water into a jug and add your yeast – stir to make sure it has dissolved. Weigh your butter and roughly divide into four, then chop each quarter into small 5mm cubes.

Add the egg mix to the dry ingredients and use a scraper or spatula to bring the dough together into a shaggy mass. Cover and rest for 20 minutes.

Turn out onto the counter and knead firmly (see page 109) or use a stand mixer with the dough hook for 10 minutes until it achieves moderate gluten development (it should be strong and elastic and pass the windowpane test – see page 110). At this point, add the first of your four portions of butter. Flatten the dough onto the counter and dot the cubes on top before folding it over to enclose. Continue kneading, using the heel of your hand. At first the dough will break apart into strands but soon the butter will be absorbed into the dough. Repeat with the remaining butter portions, waiting for each one to be fully absorbed before adding more. Once all the butter is added, your dough will be glossy and smooth with strong gluten development.

Stetch and fold your dough to form a boule (see page 113), then place in an oiled bowl, cover and place in the fridge for at least 6 hours or overnight.

Brioche loaf

Difficulty: ▢▢
Makes: 1 small loaf or
6 x 80g burger buns

Prep: 50 mins
Rest: overnight
Prove: 1–2 hrs
Bake: 25–30 mins

Equipment: 450g
loaf tin
Digital thermometer

1 x Brioche Dough
(see page 204)
Egg Wash (see
page 251)
Sesame seeds, for
sprinkling (optional)

Turning your brioche dough into a loaf is easy. The Brioche Dough recipe on page 204 is enough to make a small loaf that will fit into a 450g loaf tin. Double the recipe and use a larger tin if required.

Follow the instructions for making the brioche dough (see page 204) and refrigerate overnight.

The next day, follow the method for shaping a batard (see page 114). Grease a 450g loaf tin well and place the loaf in the tin with the seam side down. Cover the dough with oiled cling film and prove for 1–2 hours until puffy or prove in the oven (see below). The dough should slowly push back to its original shape when gently pressed with a finger.

Preheat your oven to 210°C/190°C fan/gas 6–7 with a heavy-duty baking sheet on the shelf towards the end of the prove time.

When the loaf is fully proved, egg wash the surface gently and place into the oven on the hot baking sheet. Immediately turn the oven down to 195°C/175°C fan/gas 5–6 and bake for 20 minutes. After 20 minutes, turn the loaf and cover, if necessary, with some baking parchment to stop the crust getting too dark.

Bake for another 5–10 minutes until the centre of the loaf is 97°C (use a thermometer). Cool in the tin for 15 minutes, remove and cool on a rack.

Brioche buns

Follow the instructions for making the brioche dough (see page 204) and refrigerate overnight.

The next day, divide the dough into 50–90g pieces, depending on the size of buns you want. Put the shaped buns on a lined baking tray, spaced slightly apart. You can prove your buns in the oven with just the light on and place a mug of boiling water inside to keep the humidity high.

After 50 minutes–1 hour when the buns are puffy and almost doubled in size, remove from the oven and preheat the oven to 200°C/180°C fan/gas 6.

Egg wash the buns carefully all over and sprinkle with sesame seeds, if desired. Bake for 12–15 minutes until a shiny, mahogany brown, turning the tray after 10 minutes. Cool on a rack.

Brioche doughnuts

Difficulty: ⬭ ⬭
Makes: 10 x 50g
doughnuts

Prep: 1 hr,
including frying
Rest: overnight
Prove: 2 hrs

Equipment: Deep-fat
fryer or a large
deep pan
Piping bag with a
Berliner piping tip
or a disposable
piping bag

1 x Brioche Dough
(see page 204)
1–2 litres (dependent on
pan size) sunflower oil
100g caster sugar
1 tsp ground cinnamon
(optional)

Brioche makes very special doughnuts. Raspberry Vanilla Jam (see page 239) is our most popular filling, but we can't resist dreaming up new flavours so there's always something new on the counter.

Follow the instructions for making the brioche dough (see page 204) and refrigerate overnight.

The next day, remove your dough from the fridge and divide it into 10 x 50g pieces. Flatten each piece of dough into a disc, then secure the bottom edge of the dough with the fingertips of your left hand (to stop it moving) while stretching the top edge of the dough away from you with your right hand.

Fold the stretched dough over into the centre of the disc, then turn the dough a quarter turn to the left. Repeat the stretch/fold until all sides of the dough are folded into the centre (four times in total).

Flip the dough over so it's smooth side up. Place it a little distance away from your working area and pull the dough ball towards you, tensioning it on the table as it travels. This will tighten the surface of the dough. Turn the dough 90° and repeat this action until you have formed a ball of dough with a tight skin on the surface.

Cradle your thumb and fingertips around the dough ball with the side of your hand in contact with the counter. Rotate the dough ball (sideways) within your hand, keeping the base of the dough ball in the same place – don't let it roll over. Use no flour to get surface tension on the dough ball.

Oil a baking sheet lightly, then place the doughnuts on it, spaced slightly apart and seam side down. Lightly flour their tops, cover with cling film and place in a warm place for approx. 2 hours until puffy and doubled in size. Fifteen minutes before the end of the proving time, heat your oil to 185°C in a deep-fat fryer or a large deep pan. If you're using a pan, the oil should not come further than halfway up the sides.

When your oil is ready, use your plastic scraper to lift your doughnuts from the sheet into the hot oil – take care not to create any hot oil splashes. Depending on the size of your fryer or pan, you will be doing this in batches – don't overcrowd the doughnuts. Fry for 2 minutes each side until golden brown, then use a perforated scoop to gently flip them over and fry for an additional 2 minutes. Use the scoop to take the doughnuts from the oil and place on kitchen paper to remove any excess oil.

Put the sugar in a bowl and when the doughnuts are cool enough to handle (but still warm), gently roll in the sugar mixed with the cinnamon, if using. Stack the doughnuts upright on their edges to cool before filling.

To fill the doughnuts, use a small sharp knife to create a small cut (no wider than the knife blade) in the top edge of each doughnut, then push the knife into the centre and wiggle it from side to side to open up the internal space like an upside-down V – keep the outer hole as small as possible. This will give lots of space for jam or custard but won't let it leak out.

Fill a piping bag with your chosen filling and use a Berliner piping tip or cut a 5mm hole in the end of a disposable piping bag. Hold the doughnut in one hand as you fill – it will swell and feel satisfyingly heavier! We aim for 50g of filling in each doughnut.

Rhubarb and custard doughnuts

Difficulty: 🍩🍩
Makes: 10 x 50g doughnuts

Prep: 40 mins
Cool: 30 mins

10 x ready-to-fill
  Brioche Doughnuts
  (see page 208)
Vanilla Custard
  (for Doughnuts)
  (see page 255)
Sugar, for dusting

Rhubarb compote
300g rhubarb (forced
  or green)
200g caster sugar
5g cornflour
1 tbsp water

Poached rhubarb batons
200g forced rhubarb
Juice of 1 orange
30g caster sugar

School dinners, jars of hard-boiled sweets and the daft antics of a cartoon cat and dog make this pairing an irresistible trip down memory lane. As you bite through the sugar-coated brioche, the tangy rhubarb provides a perfect contrast to the cool, creamy custard.

Use the brioche base recipe. Shape, prove and fry your doughnuts as before, then fill with rhubarb compote and vanilla custard and decorate with poached rhubarb.

To make the rhubarb compote, cut the stalks into 2cm pieces of equal thickness and place in a pan with the sugar. Simmer until the liquid in the rhubarb has reduced, then mix the cornflour to a paste with the water and mix into the hot fruit. Simmer briefly until thickened, then cool.

To poach the rhubarb, trim the ends and cut into batons on the diagonal, 3cm long and 2cm wide. Place the rhubarb pieces in a deep baking dish so that each piece can sit in the poaching liquid. Juice the orange and pour the liquid into a small pan. Add the sugar, bring to the boil, then pour the liquid over the prepared rhubarb and cover the dish with cling film or a lid to retain the heat so that the rhubarb gently poaches. Keep checking the rhubarb and remove it from the liquid as soon as it feels soft. Allow the rhubarb to cool on a rack, then store in the fridge.

Toss your fried doughnuts in sugar before cooling and filling. Fill two piping bags, one with rhubarb compote and the other with vanilla custard. Follow the instructions for filling your doughnuts on page 209, using the compote first and leaving space to complete the fill with the vanilla custard. Top each doughnut with a few pieces of poached rhubarb.

Apple cinnamon doughnuts

Difficulty: ⬚ ⬚
Makes: 10 x 50g
   doughnuts

Prep: 40 mins
Cool: 30 mins

10 x ready-to-fill
   Brioche Doughnuts
   (see page 208)
200g Granny Smith
   apples
200g Bramley apples
200g Pink Lady/
   Braeburn apples
200g caster sugar
50ml water
½ recipe Vanilla Custard
   (for Doughnuts) (see
   page 255)
1 tbsp ground cinnamon
Bay Sugar (see page
   199), for decoration

A sharper, fruity filling, sprinkled with bay sugar to finish. Use the brioche base recipe. Shape, prove and fry your doughnuts as before, then fill with apple custard.

To make the apple filling, peel, core and finely dice the apples and combine with 50g of the sugar and the water in a heavy-based pan. Bring to a low simmer over a medium-high heat, then reduce the heat, cover and simmer, stirring occasionally, for 10 minutes, until the apple breaks down.

Remove the lid and continue to stir over a medium heat until the mixture is slightly dry and thick and when you pull a spoon across the bottom of the pan, the mix does not flow back straight away. Process the apple in a blender or press through a sieve until smooth.

Cool the apple mix, then fold two-thirds into a half portion of the vanilla custard and refrigerate until required. The remaining apple mix will be used to decorate your filled doughnut.

Mix the remaining sugar with the ground cinnamon and toss your fried doughnuts in the sugar mix before cooling and filling. To fill your doughnuts, whisk the apple custard to loosen and follow the filling instructions on page 209. Decorate with a spoonful of the apple mix and a sprinkle of bay sugar.

Caramel custard doughnuts

Difficulty: ☐ ☐
Makes: 10 x 50g
doughnuts

Prep: 40 mins
Cool: 30 mins

Equipment: Digital
thermometer

10 x ready-to-fill
Brioche Doughnuts
(see page 208)
175ml full-fat milk
150ml double cream
1 egg yolk
1 egg
20g cornflour
40g light brown sugar
Sugar, for dusting
Salted Honeycomb
Crunch (see page 258)

Honeycomb caramel
90g caster sugar
40g golden syrup
or honey
20ml water
½ tsp bicarbonate
of soda
Flaky sea salt

Standing at the sink, washing up a honeycomb-encrusted pan and watching the caramel dissolve in hot water provided the inspiration for this recipe. Follow the custard base recipe, substituting brown sugar, then dissolve the honeycomb caramel into the hot milk.

Use the brioche base recipe. Shape, prove and fry your doughnuts as before, then fill. Decorate each doughnut with a chunk or two of Salted Honeycomb Crunch (see page 258).

Place the milk and half the cream in a pan and heat until steaming, but not boiling. Remove from the heat while you make the honeycomb caramel.

Take a large, deep saucepan, add the sugar, syrup or honey and water and boil the sugar mix until it reaches 150°C. Remove from the heat, then add the bicarbonate of soda – be prepared by covering your hands with oven gloves as the caramel will bubble up and the steam can burn! Continue to whisk the bubbling caramel off the heat until it darkens to a rich, golden caramel. Add a pinch of the sea salt, then pour over the warm milk mix and stir to dissolve.

Put the egg yolk, whole egg, cornflour and light brown sugar in a bowl and whisk to a smooth paste. Pour the hot milk and caramel liquid over the egg mixture and stir to combine.

Add the liquid back into the pan and place over a low heat, stirring constantly with a whisk or spatula to ensure no lumps form. When the custard thickens (enough to draw a finger through it on the back of a spatula) or reaches 75°C, add the remaining double cream and whisk together. Pour into a bowl and press some cling film onto the custard surface to prevent a skin forming. Cool, then place in the fridge and use fully chilled within 3 days.

Toss your fried doughnuts in sugar before cooling and filling. To fill your doughnuts, whisk the custard to loosen and follow the instructions on page 209. Decorate with a chunk or two of the honeycomb crunch.

Cardamom knots

Difficulty: ▢ ▢
Makes: 12

Prep: 1 hr
Rest: 20 mins
Prove: 2–3 hrs
Chill: 20 mins
Bake: 12–15 mins

Equipment: Large metal muffin tray

Cardamom dough
450g strong white
  bread flour
80g icing sugar, sifted
12g ground cardamom
8g fine sea salt
75g cold unsalted
  butter, cubed
260g full-fat milk
7g active dried yeast

Cardamom butter
100g soft unsalted butter
80g caster sugar
10g ground cardamom
10g lemon juice
⅛ tsp fine sea salt

To finish
Egg Wash (see
  page 251)
50g nibbed sugar
Stock Syrup (see
  page 259)

I really recommend you try and source black cardamom seeds, grinding them fresh for every bake. Their intense, astringent taste is utterly unique. Once tasted it will live in your memory and keep you returning, again and again.

Weigh the flour, icing sugar, cardamom and salt into a large bowl and mix to combine. Rub the cubed butter into the flour mix until it resembles fine breadcrumbs. Warm the milk to the correct temperature (see page 108), add the yeast and stir to dissolve. Add this liquid to the dry mix and bring the dough together using your scraper until all the dry matter is incorporated.

Allow the dough to rest in the bowl, covered, for 20 minutes, then turn out onto the counter and knead for 5 minutes until you have a smooth, elastic dough (see page 109). Place the dough back in the bowl, cover and prove for 1 hour with stretch and folds after 20 and 40 minutes (see page 113). Maintain the dough temperature at 26°C.

While your dough is proving, make the cardamom butter by gently combining all the ingredients in a bowl.

Roll the dough into a 60cm x 24cm rectangle, with the narrowest side next to your body. Spread with the cardamom butter and fold the bottom edge halfway to the centre of the dough, then fold the top edge of the dough to fully cover the first half of the dough (a single/letter fold). The dough will now measure 20cm x 24cm.

Wrap the dough in cling film or baking parchment and chill in the freezer for 20 minutes. Remove and place the longest side of the dough parallel to your body. Gently roll the chilled dough to 30cm high, then trim the sides. Cut 12 x 2cm wide strips of dough. Cut each strip into three sections from the bottom edge, leaving the top edge still attached so that each strip has three sections. Prepare your tin by greasing it well or lining with cases.

Plait the sections and roll each plaited strip so that the ends are tucked underneath when placed into the muffin tin. Prove for 1–2 hours until puffy and increased in size.

Preheat the oven to 200°C/180°C fan/gas 6.

Brush the buns with egg wash and sprinkle with nibbed sugar, then bake for 12–15 minutes. Brush liberally with syrup as soon as they are out of the oven, then turn out of the tin after 10 minutes to prevent the buns sticking.

Cardamom buns with redcurrants, raspberry, rose and pistachio

Difficulty: ◻ ◻
Makes: 10

Prep: 1 hr
Prove: 2–3 hrs
Bake: 12–15 mins

1 x Cardamom Dough
  (see page 218)
Vanilla Custard
  (for Doughnuts)
  (see page 255)
250g raspberries
125g redcurrants
Egg Wash (see
  page 251)
200g icing sugar
1 tbsp rose water
100g pistachios,
  finely chopped
2 tbsp raspberry jam
  (optional)

These tasty morning buns use our cardamom dough base recipe. Source the greenest pistachios you can find – their colour looks stunning with juicy red summer berries.

Prepare the vanilla custard so that it has time to cool before use.

Make the cardamom dough and prove for 1 hour with stretch and folds at 20 and 40 minutes. Divide into 10 x 50g pieces. Shape each piece of dough into a loose boule (see page 113) and place it onto a baking tray lined with baking parchment, leaving space for the buns to expand as they prove.

Prove the buns for 1–2 hours until light and puffy.

Preheat the oven to 195°C/175°C fan/gas 5–6.

Just before baking, use two fingers to depress the dough in the centre of each bun, creating a flat area approximately 5cm in diameter. Fill this space with cold custard, then top with half the raspberries and all the redcurrants.

Egg wash the edges of the dough and bake the buns for 12–15 minutes until golden brown, turning the tray after 10 minutes.

Once the buns are cool, mix the icing sugar with the rose water and enough cold water to make a thick water icing. Use a teaspoon to drip the icing around the rim of each bun, then sprinkle with the pistachios and the remaining raspberries. Brush with a little jam, warmed in a small pan, for a glossy finish.

Queenie

Difficulty: ○

Prep: 15 mins *(if you have already laminated the dough)*
Prove: 1½–2 hrs
Bake: 12–15 mins

Equipment: Individual 10cm round metal tins or a metal muffin tray (using metal is important to ensure the caramel is hard) If you have a lot of trimmings, you could make a giant queenie using a solid-sided cake tin – just make sure it doesn't have a loose bottom!

Soft unsalted butter, to liberally cover the sides and base of the tins/muffin tray
Sugar, equal to the amount of butter
Croissant dough trimmings (enough to cover the base of the tin) (see page 182)
Egg Wash (see page 251)
Flaky sea salt

While not winning any prizes in the looks department, this hack version of the magnificent kouign amann pastry (pronounced 'Queen Aman') is a great way to use up your trimmings. As the pastry bakes, molten butter and sugar create a pool of salted caramel. Remove from the tin while they're hot before they stick fast. The result: a tender puck of buttery pastry with a salty-sweet, crisply caramelised bottom.

I've been quite loose with the amounts of butter and sugar you'll need as it depends on the size of your tin. Remember, you're essentially making caramel underneath your dough – don't be stingy!

Grease your tins/muffin tray liberally with butter – cover the sides and make sure there's plenty of butter left for the base. Sprinkle sugar liberally over the sides of the tins/tray and a generous amount over the base. You could experiment with blending brown and white sugars for an even darker caramel.

Chop your dough trimmings into pieces approx. 3cm square and arrange them over the butter/sugar mix – enough to cover the base and approx. 3cm high.

Preheat the oven to 195°C/175°C fan/gas 5–6.

Allow the queenies to prove for 1½–2 hours until jiggly along with your other pastries (see page 182). Egg wash and bake for 12–15 minutes, turning the tins/tray after 10 minutes and following the croissant method (see page 182) until the queenies are a glossy, deep golden brown.

Once out of the oven, cool for 5 minutes, then remove from the tins/tray and place on a rack, bottom side up. Sprinkle with a little flaky sea salt.

Almond toast

Difficulty: ⏲

Prep: 30 mins
Bake: 25–40 mins

Equipment: Loaf tin
suitable for your
dough weight
Digital thermometer

Croissant dough
trimmings (approx.
500g) (see page 182)
Egg Wash (see
page 251)
Stock Syrup (see page
259), made with a
dash of rum (optional)
Flaked almonds,
for scattering
Icing sugar, for dusting

Frangipane
125g soft unsalted butter
200g caster sugar
50g egg whites
2 eggs
250g ground almonds
½ tsp almond extract
1 tsp rum (optional)

The lovechild of an almond croissant and a brioche bostock, almond toast is already proved and baked so only needs a short blast in the oven until the sweet smell of toasted almonds is wafting through your house. You can keep your trimmings in the freezer each time you make a batch of dough until you have enough for a loaf. Alternatively, this recipe works really well using a brioche loaf instead for the base.

Grease your loaf tin well, paying attention to the corners of the tin. Flour your counter generously, bunch your trimmings together and then roll the jumbled-up dough into a rectangle slightly less than the width of your loaf tin and three times the length. Try not to have any large holes but perfection isn't necessary here – this is a very forgiving bake!

Take the top edge of the rectangle and roll it tightly towards you. Place the rolled dough, seam side down, into the tin and egg wash the surface. Prove for 1–2 hours until puffed up and jiggly, then preheat your oven to 195°C/175°C fan/gas 5–6 and bake for 15–25 minutes (depending on the weight of the dough) until deep golden brown. Use your thermometer to check the centre is 97°C or a skewer inserted into the centre comes out clean. Cool the loaf in the tin until cool enough to handle, then remove from the tin and place on a cooling rack.

While your loaf is cooling, make the frangipane by gently beating the butter and sugar together, without incorporating too much air. Gently beat in the egg whites and eggs, then add the ground almonds, almond extract and rum, if using.

Make your stock syrup following the instructions on page 259, adding a dash of rum for flavour if you like.

Allow the loaf to cool completely before slicing into 1.5cm slices. Brush one side of each slice with stock syrup, then generously spread with the frangipane using the back of a spoon or palette knife.

Finish with a generous scattering of flaked almonds, pressing them down lightly. You can freeze the slices at this stage or bake at 195°C/175°C fan/gas 5–6 for 10–12 minutes until golden brown – watch the colour of those flaked almonds closely towards the end of the bake! Allow to cool slightly before dusting generously with icing sugar and serving straight away.

Almond croissants

Difficulty: ⏲

Prep: 30 mins
Bake: 10–12 mins

Leftover Croissants
(see page 180) or
Pain au Chocolat
(see page 186)
Stock Syrup (see
page 259)
Frangipane (see
opposite)
Flaked almonds,
for scattering
Icing sugar, for dusting

The forerunner of almond toast, it's the worst-kept secret in the bakery world that unsold croissants are reincarnated as something greater than the sum of their original parts. They really are the gift that just keeps on giving! These freeze well, so stash some away next time you have leftovers!

Preheat your oven to 195°C/175°C fan/gas 5–6.

Slice your baked croissants in half horizontally (tip to tip), then brush both cut sides with your stock syrup. Spread the frangipane generously over the lower cut side, sandwich the top half in place, then spread some more frangipane over the top. Sprinkle the frangipane top with flaked almonds, then freeze or place on a baking tray and bake for 10–12 minutes until golden brown – watch the colour of the flaked almonds closely towards the end of the bake! Cool slightly before dusting generously with icing sugar and serve straight away.

These can be baked directly from frozen – allow a couple of extra minutes in the oven and check that the centre is fully baked before serving.

The
Larder

Making jam, chutney and pickles is a great way of using up a glut of seasonal fruit so you can continue to enjoy the flavours throughout the year. You'll feel a warm glow of satisfaction every time you see those jars gleaming at the back of your cupboard or when you're showered with praise by grateful friends and family.

We use jam in quite a few of our recipes – especially our brioche doughnuts – and always make sure it's the same jam served in our cafés and for sale in the shops.

Larder notes

Sugar

Granulated sugar is best for jam-making as the grains dissolve slowly and evenly so there's less chance of them burning on the bottom of the pan. Their larger surface area also means fewer grains, so less scum on your jam as it boils. Granulated sugar with added pectin is also available – you could use this in recipes where the natural pectin level of the fruit is low instead of adding pectin powder.

Pectin

We use a small amount of pectin powder in jams made with fruit naturally low in pectin. Purists might turn up their noses at this, but if you've ever accidentally made jam that just slides off your toast, you'll know where I'm coming from. You can also thicken jam by cooking it for longer, but it will be much sweeter and the bright colour will be lost. Pectin powder is widely available and is made from powdered apples – nothing else!

Wrinkle test

Place a small flat plate in your fridge when you start. Once your jam reaches 105°C, drip about ½ teaspoon onto the cold plate. Let it cool for a minute, then gently push it inwards with your fingertip. If the surface wrinkles, then your jam is set. If not, continue to boil and repeat the test every few minutes as the jam continues to boil.

Macerating

If you have the time, let the fruit juices dissolve the sugar overnight. There's less risk of the sugar catching on the bottom of the pan and the time taken to reach the set point will be quicker, so the colour will stay vibrant. By then straining the fruit and just boiling the juices and sugar you will retain the texture of the fruit.

Sterilising jam jars

It's important to sterilise your jars properly so that you remove any bacteria that could cause mould growth. Wash the jars and lids in hot, soapy water, rinse well, then place on a clean baking tray and put into a preheated 180°C/160°C fan/gas 4 oven for 20 minutes. Turn off the oven, but leave the jars inside so they are still warm when you ladle in the jam/chutney. The jam/chutney should fill the jar, leaving a 1–2cm gap at the top. Place a baking parchment disc or a pre-cut cellophane circle on top of the jam/chutney to prevent mould growth. Screw the lid on the jar while the jam/chutney is hot.

JAM/CHUTNEY-MAKING EQUIPMENT

- Digital thermometer

- Slotted spoon

- Lidded jam jars

- Baking parchment/cellophane discs

Strawberry rose jam

Difficulty: 🍞 🍞
Makes: 4 x 200g jars

Prep: 30 mins
Macerating: overnight
Cook: 30 mins

500g strawberries,
 ripe and flavourful
450g granulated sugar
1 tsp pectin powder
Juice of ½ lemon
3 tsp rose water

I made this jam after tasting rose petal jam while on holiday in Turkey and, unable to resist anything floral, wanted to create something similar (but more attainable!). I gave a jar to my neighbour and she still reminds me of it to this day. Sue, this one's for you.

The day before, quickly rinse the strawberries in cold water, then hull them, slicing any that are very large in half but keeping the majority whole if possible. Place the strawberries, sugar, pectin, lemon juice and rose water into a large pan and bring this mixture to a brief simmer. Remove from the heat, cover and leave to macerate overnight.

The next day, place a small plate in your fridge to chill. Strain the macerated strawberries through a sieve and pour the juices into a large, heavy-based pan. Retain the fruit until later. Bring the juices to the boil, stirring regularly to eliminate hot spots. Skim the surface as required with a slotted spoon and continue until the temperature reaches 105°C, then add the strawberries to the pan.

Return to the boil until 105°C is reached again. Check the set using the wrinkle test (see page 231), then remove from the heat and ladle into warmed sterilised jam jars (see page 231), tapping them slightly on the counter to ensure there are no air gaps. Seal and lid the jars.

Yellow plum, orange and cardamom jam

GF

Difficulty: ⬭⬭
Makes: 5 x 200g jars

Prep: 30 mins
Macerating: overnight
Cook: 50 mins

1 large orange
100g caster sugar
100ml water
500g small plums
  or greengages
400g granulated sugar
Juice of ½ lemon
1 tsp black cardamom
  seeds, ground

There are so many opportunities for foraging in this country – keep your eye out for wild blossom in the spring so you know where to look in late summer. Walking through my village, I spotted tiny orange plums so densely scattered on the ground outside a house it looked like a children's ball pond. The branches drooped with the promise of more to come. Once I'd got the go-ahead, the ground seemed like the best place to start. The coverage was such that it was impossible not to step on the fruit, releasing a sweetly rotting smell from plums buried deep. I was accompanied by the occasional 'ding' as fruit fell on the car below – apparently an irritant to the homeowners who'd never tried the bounty on their doorstep. I made many return visits, even taking some jam for my benefactors. I'm secretly hoping they're not converted so I can enjoy those plums next year!

The day before, wash the orange thoroughly in warm water, then, using a sharp knife, slice into 5mm rings. Slice the rings into small dice, then place the juice, peel and flesh (removing any pips) into a pan with the caster sugar and water. Poach at a low simmer until the orange peel becomes translucent, about 30 minutes. Top up the water if required.

Meanwhile, wash the plums in cold water and cut each one in half to remove the stone. Place the prepared plums in a large pan with the granulated sugar, lemon juice and cardamom. Add the prepared orange peel and the remaining poaching liquid. Bring the plum/orange mix to a brief simmer, then remove from the heat, cover and leave the jam to macerate overnight.

The next day, place a small plate in your fridge to chill. Bring the fruit to the boil, stirring regularly to eliminate hot spots. Skim the surface as required with a slotted spoon and continue to boil for 5–10 minutes until the temperature reaches 105°C. Check the set using the wrinkle test (see page 231), then remove from the heat and ladle into warmed sterilised jam jars (see page 231), tapping them slightly on the counter to ensure there are no air gaps, then seal and lid.

Cherry amaretto jam

Difficulty: 🍞🍞
Makes: 4 x 200g jars

Prep: 30 mins
Macerating: overnight
Cook: 20 mins

500g cherries, frozen
  or fresh
250g granulated sugar
Juice of ½ lemon
60ml amaretto liqueur
1 tsp pectin powder
½ tsp mahleb, finely
  ground, or almond
  extract

This gorgeous jam is perfect for a special occasion or as a gift to someone who you know will appreciate it. There's a beautiful circularity with this flavour combination (think Bakewell tart) as cherry pits (and other stone fruit such as bitter almonds and apricots) are a source of benzaldehyde, which is the flavour compound associated with almond extract and amaretto liqueur.

Sticking with the theme, mahleb is a powder made from the seed of a St Lucy's cherry and gives a unique almond/vanilla flavour to many Mediterranean cakes and pastries.

The cherry season in this country is short – frozen cherries will give you a similar outcome.

This jam could be used in the base of the Chocolate Amaretto Tart (see page 89) or served on French toast with a dollop of mascarpone and some chocolate shavings (see page 28).

The day before making the jam, wash the cherries in cold water (if they're fresh) and cut each one in half to remove the pit. Defrost the frozen cherries if using. Place the cherries in a large pan with the sugar, lemon juice, amaretto, pectin powder and mahleb/almond extract. Bring the cherry mix to a brief simmer, then remove from the heat, cover and leave to macerate overnight.

The next day, place a small plate in your fridge to chill. Bring the fruit to the boil, stirring regularly to eliminate hot spots. Skim the surface as required with a slotted spoon and continue to boil for 5–10 minutes until the temperature reaches 105°C. Check the set using the wrinkle test (see page 231), then remove from the heat and ladle into warmed sterilised jam jars (see page 231), tapping them slightly on the counter to ensure there are no air gaps, then seal and lid.

GF

Raspberry vanilla jam

Difficulty: ⬚⬚
Makes: 4 x 200g jars

Prep: 30 mins
Macerating: overnight
Cook: 20 mins

500g raspberries
1 vanilla pod
400g granulated sugar
Juice of ½ lemon

If you've ever taken the time to smell a punnet of warm, fresh raspberries, you'll know the perfume is candyfloss sweet, fruity and floral, though it's not surprising as they're a member of the rose family. The raspberry season is short and as the weather changes, new varieties, each with a distinct flavour, are available from increasingly northern parts of the country. Keep an eye on the price in your local market or fruit farms and buy your raspberries when the price is right. When you open the jar, months later, you'll be transported back to a time of open windows, blue skies and sunshine – your kitchen rich with their heady smell.

Pick over the raspberries to check for quality, but don't wash them. Use a sharp knife to split the vanilla pod in half lengthways and scrape out the seeds into a heavy-based pan.

Add the raspberries, sugar and lemon juice. Chop the scraped vanilla pod into quarters and add these. Bring this mixture to a brief simmer, then remove from the heat, cover and leave to macerate overnight.

The next day, place a small plate in your fridge to chill. Bring the fruit to the boil, stirring regularly to eliminate hot spots. Skim the surface as required with a slotted spoon and continue to boil for 5–10 minutes until the temperature reaches 105°C. Check the set using the wrinkle test (see page 231), then remove from the heat and ladle into warmed sterilised jam jars (see page 231), adding a piece of vanilla pod to each jar and tapping them slightly on the counter to ensure there are no air gaps, then seal and lid.

Rhubarb and ginger jam

Difficulty: ⌷⌷
Makes: 5 x 200g jars

Prep: 30 mins
Macerating: overnight
Cook: 30 mins

500g rhubarb, trimmed
    weight
500g granulated sugar
1 tsp pectin powder
Juice of ½ lemon
10g fresh ginger,
    peeled and
    finely grated
40g stem ginger,
    chopped into
    small dice
½ tsp beetroot
    powder (optional)

This sharp and peppery jam looks at its prettiest when early pink rhubarb is in the shops, though late season rhubarb is just as delicious. If desired, just add a little beetroot powder to bring the colour back.

Rinse the rhubarb in cold water and cut the stalks in half lengthways, then into 2–3cm batons. Mix and macerate the rhubarb, sugar, pectin, lemon juice and fresh ginger overnight in a covered non-metallic bowl.

The next day, strain the macerated fruit through a sieve and pour the juices into a large, heavy-based pan. Retain the fruit until later. Place a small plate in your fridge to chill. Bring the juices to the boil, stirring regularly to eliminate hot spots. Skim the surface as required with a slotted spoon and continue cooking until the temperature reaches 105°C (approx. 15–20 minutes) and it has passed the wrinkle test (see page 231). Once a good set has been achieved, add the reserved fruit, the stem ginger and beetroot powder (if using) and briefly return to 105°C.

Remove from the heat and ladle into warmed sterilised jam jars (see page 231), tapping them slightly on the counter to ensure there are no air gaps, then seal and lid.

GF

Jalapeño pickles

Difficulty: ▢ ▢
Makes: 3 x 200g jars

Prep: 15 mins
Pickling: 1 day
Cook: 2 mins

250g jalapeño peppers
(weight before
removing stalks)
150ml white wine
vinegar
40ml water
150g caster sugar
20g fine sea salt

One night we'd been trialling a new baguette recipe and needed to slice a couple open to check the crumb. A quick rummage in the fridge unearthed these piquant pickles, waiting to be used in our chilli bread, and some slices of tasty smoked ham for tomorrow's sandwiches. It was the most perfect midnight picnic – a jambon beurre with a twist!

These pickles are ready to eat the next day but will keep for up to a month in their pickling liquid.

Remove the stalks from the peppers and slice thinly into 3mm-thick rounds (it's not necessary to deseed the peppers). Place in warmed sterilised jars (see page 231) or a clean lidded container.

Place the vinegar, water, caster sugar and salt into a pan and heat gently until the sugar and salt are dissolved fully – around 2 minutes.

Pour the hot pickling liquid over the sliced peppers. Leave to cool, then cover and store in your fridge or a cool, dark place.

Balsamic fig chutney

Difficulty: ⬚ ⬚
Makes: 3 x 200g jars

Prep: 30 mins
Soaking: 2 hrs or
  overnight
Cook: 50 mins

300g dried figs
2 tbsp sunflower
  oil
75g red onion,
  finely diced
½ tsp ground
  cinnamon
½ tsp ground
  nutmeg
1 tsp mixed spice
½ tsp fine sea salt
125g Bramley apple,
  peeled, cored
  and chopped
  (chopped weight)
125g dark brown sugar
50ml red wine vinegar
75ml balsamic vinegar

This stuff is unctuously addictive – sweet and savoury in the same bite and perfect with oozy, ripe cheese or a wedge of Cheddar.

Place the dried figs in a heatproof bowl and cover with boiling water. Leave to soak for a couple of hours (or overnight), then drain, reserving 75ml of the soaking water for later.

The next day, heat the oil in a large, heavy-based pan and gently cook the onion to soften. Add the spices and salt and fry until toasted and fragrant.

Remove the stalks from the soaked figs and chop them each into four pieces. Add to the pan with the apple and the 75ml of reserved fig water. Simmer gently for 30 minutes with a lid on the pan, stirring regularly.

Add the sugar and vinegars and simmer for about 15–20 minutes until the chutney is pulpy and no longer watery.

Ladle into warmed sterilised jam jars (see page 231), tapping them slightly on the counter to ensure there are no air gaps, then seal and lid.

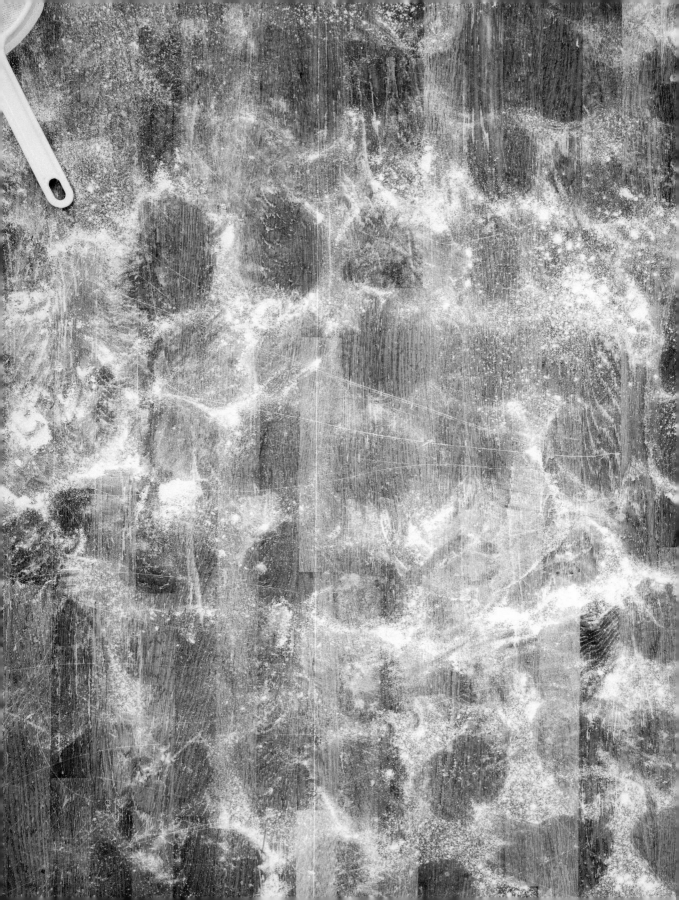

Base
Recipes

Sweet pastry

Difficulty: ⊓ ⊓
**Makes: enough to line
2 x 20cm tart tins**

**Prep: 30 mins
Chill: before using**

380g plain flour
120g icing sugar
180g cold unsalted
    butter
40g water
40g egg yolks (2 eggs)

**Use this recipe to make a beautiful crisp tart case – the perfect,
prepare-ahead centrepiece for a special dessert. Make it rustic
with frangipane and tumbled stone fruit or pretty as a picture with
thickened pastry cream (see pages 254–255) and summer berries.**

Sift the flour into a bowl or onto a counter with the icing sugar and a pinch
of fine sea salt. Chop the cold butter into cubes approximately 1cm square
and add **(1)**. Use your fingertips or a dough scraper to rub the butter into
the flour mix until small breadcrumbs size (or beat slowly with the paddle
attachment of a stand mixer) **(2)**.

In a small bowl, lightly whisk the water and egg yolks together, then add this
gradually to the butter/flour mix. Bring the mix together with your hands,
a fork or slowly with the paddle and stop mixing as soon as it starts to
form a ball **(3)**.

Knead the dough very briefly on the counter to press and push the dough
into a block no more than 2cm thick – this will make subsequent rolling
out easier **(4)**. Wrap tightly in cling film or baking parchment and chill in
the fridge before using.

Chocolate sweet pastry

Difficulty: ☐ ☐

**Makes: enough to line
2 x 20cm tart tins**

....

Prep: 30 mins

Chill: before using

....

360g plain flour

120g icing sugar

20g cocoa powder

180g cold unsalted
   butter

40g cold water

40g egg yolks (2 eggs)

This recipe freezes well, so cut the block in half, wrap well and keep for next time. The colour of this pastry makes it hard to know when it's cooked, so remember to set a timer and use your other senses – touch and smell.

Sift the flour into a bowl or onto a counter with the icing sugar, cocoa powder and a pinch of fine sea salt. Chop the cold butter into cubes approximately 1cm square and add. Use your fingertips or a dough scraper to rub the butter into the flour mix until small breadcrumbs size (or beat slowly with the paddle attachment of a stand mixer).

In a small bowl, lightly whisk the cold water and egg yolks together, then add this gradually to the butter/flour mix. Bring the mix together with your hands, a fork or slowly with the paddle and stop mixing as soon as it starts to form a ball.

Knead the dough very briefly on the counter to press and push the dough into a block no more than 2cm thick – this will make subsequent rolling out easier. Wrap tightly in cling film or baking parchment and chill in the fridge before using.

Puff pastry

Difficulty: ○○○
Makes: 1kg

Prep: 2-day process
   with 1½ hrs active time

310g strong white
   bread flour
310g plain flour
15g fine sea salt
60g cold unsalted butter
280g cold water
20g white wine or
   cider vinegar
250g cold unsalted
   butter (for lamination)

**TIPS FOR BAKING
PUFF PASTRY**

• Don't roll the dough any
thinner than 5mm or the
butter will no longer be
held in separate layers
and will start merging
with the dough.

• When baking, start with
a high heat, then turn
your oven down after
10 minutes.

• Don't open your oven
door for the first 75% of
your bake. The water in
the butter turns to steam
in the heat of the oven,
forcing each layer apart.
Once forced apart, the
butter cooks each layer
of dough – crisping it
separately. If the oven
door is opened, the layers
deflate as the steam
rushes out, causing the
layers to collapse.

Puff pastry follows a similar laminating method to the Croissant dough on page 181. The water content of the butter, folded into the dough, puffs up the pastry with steam in the heat of the oven, creating hundreds of light and airy layers. Although this dough takes time to complete, the actual processes are simple and quick, so don't be daunted by it – most of the time is fridge time, not yours. Puff pastry freezes really well, so it's worth making double.

Day 1: Weigh your flours and salt into a large bowl. Combine using a whisk or the rounded edge of your scraper. Chop your butter into small chunks, then rub into the flour mix until it resembles fine breadcrumbs.

Combine the cold water with the vinegar and pour over the dry ingredients. Use your scraper to scoop, chop and mix the dough. Repeat until all the flour is mixed in and a rough dough has formed.

If you're using a stand mixer, use a dough hook on slow speed to bring the dough together. Stop when the flour is mixed in and a rough dough forms.

Cover the dough and rest for 30 minutes at room temperature, then tip out onto the counter and knead for 3–5 minutes until you have a smooth, strong dough that passes the windowpane test for moderate gluten development (see page 110). Form into a flattish rectangle and either wrap tightly in greased cling film or use a lidded greased tub. Refrigerate overnight.

Day 2: Create a butter block and encase it in the puff pastry dough following the instructions for the Croissant dough on page 181.

Folding: Roll the dough/butter parcel out to 60cm long – keeping the width approximately 20cm – then complete a single (letter) fold by folding down the top edge to just over the middle, then folding up the bottom edge to enclose the first fold.

For fold 2, turn the dough so that the long-folded edge is vertical (right or left) and reroll the dough to 60cm long by 20cm wide. Complete another single fold, then wrap your dough in plastic. I use a whiteboard marker to write the number of folds on the outside. Refrigerate so the gluten can relax.

For folds 3–4, repeat folds 1 and 2. Chill for 1 hour. For folds 5–6, repeat folds 1 and 2. After you have completed all the folds, let your dough relax for at least 1 hour or overnight before rolling out for your intended recipe.

Flaky pastry

Difficulty: ▢ ▢
**Makes: enough to line
2 x 25cm tart tins**

Prep: 30 mins
Chill: 2 hrs or overnight

330g plain flour
200g cold unsalted
  butter
¼ tsp fine sea salt
100g very cold water

**This recipe makes double the amount of flaky pastry needed for one
tart. Divide into two after making, wrap both pieces and put one in the
fridge to chill and the other in the freezer for next time.**

Sift the flour into a large bowl and chop the butter into small 2cm cubes,
handling it as little as possible to keep it cold. Toss the butter in the flour,
then use a metal dough scraper or a couple of round-bladed knives to
cut the butter into the flour until it is in large pea-sized pieces (or use the
beater attachment on your stand mixer).

Add the salt and pour the water slowly into the flour mix, stirring with
the scraper or knives (or the stand mixer and beater attachment) until the
dough comes together. You will still be able to see streaks of butter.

Divide the dough into two, then press each piece of dough together to form
a 3cm high disc. Wrap both discs in cling film to keep airtight and place in
the fridge and/or freezer for a couple of hours (or overnight).

GF

Egg wash

Difficulty: ▢
Prep: 5 mins

1 egg
1 tbsp milk

**Brushing the surface of your enriched breads, pastries and tarts with
an egg wash will give them a shiny, golden-brown finish. It will also
help sugar, spices, nuts or flaky sea salt to stay in place. This recipe
can be increased easily, depending on how much you are coating.**

Break the egg into a bowl. Add the cold milk and whisk with a fork until the
egg is fully dispersed. Use a pastry brush to gently apply your egg wash.

Vanilla genoise cake

Difficulty: 🍞 🍞
Makes: 2 x 20cm cakes

Prep: 40 mins
Bake: 30–40 mins
Cool: 30 mins

Equipment: 2 x 20cm
x 5cm round cake tins
Digital thermometer

240g plain (or gluten-free) flour
1 tsp baking powder
8 eggs
240g caster sugar
100g unsalted butter
1 tsp vanilla extract

This delicious and versatile sponge cake is quick and easy to make once you've mastered the method. Warming the eggs and sugar creates a stable foam that raises the sponge and both plain and gluten-free flours work well. We use this recipe for many of our celebration cakes – it's a wonderful blank canvas for seasonal jams and curds, flavoured syrups, creamy icing, fresh flowers and foliage.

Preheat your oven to 195°C/175°C fan/gas 5–6. Prepare your cake tins by greasing and lining the bases with baking parchment but leaving the sides of the tins grease-free.

Sift the flour, baking powder and a pinch of fine sea salt together twice.

Make a bain-marie by selecting a heatproof bowl that is slightly larger than your saucepan. Fill the saucepan with an inch of water and place over a medium heat. Place the eggs and sugar in the bowl and set it on top of the saucepan, so that it doesn't touch the simmering water below. Use a hand whisk to beat the egg and sugar mix while it's heating up.

Once the egg mix reaches 40°C, move the bowl to a stand mixer or use electric beaters and continue to whisk until pale, thick and trebled in volume – this could take up to 15 minutes.

While the eggs are whisking, melt the butter and vanilla extract. Remove the bowl from the stand mixer and add a couple of tablespoons of the foam to the melted butter and stir together briefly.

In three or four additions, quickly fold the flour mix into the remaining egg foam using a sieve to distribute it. Use a spatula in alternating figure-of-8 motions, removing any lumps but not overworking the batter – this aerated egg mix leavens the cake! Once all the flour is incorporated, fold in the thickened butter, then pour the batter into the two tins.

Bake for 30–40 minutes. The sponge is ready when the surface is dry and a skewer inserted into the centre of the cakes comes out clean. Allow the cakes to cool for 30 minutes, then run a small sharp knife around the inside edge of the tins to release the cakes. Cool on a rack.

The un-iced cakes will keep for up to 3 days if wrapped well as soon as they are completely cool. They can also be frozen.

GF

Vanilla custard base

Difficulty: ◻ ◻
Makes: 380g custard

....

Prep: 20 mins

....

175ml milk
75ml double cream
40g caster sugar
1 tbsp vanilla extract
30g egg yolk (1 egg)
30g egg (½ egg)
15g cornflour

Use this base recipe for the flavoured custards that follow.

Heat the milk, cream, sugar and vanilla in a small pan until lightly steaming.

Whisk the yolk, whole egg and cornflour in a heatproof bowl until smooth, then pour the steaming milk over. Gently whisk, then return the mixture back to the pan over a low heat, stirring constantly.

Start stirring with a spatula to keep lifting the custard off the bottom and sides of the pan (this is where it will stick first). As it starts to thicken, turn off the heat and use the whisk (and some elbow grease) to create a thick, smooth custard. Once thick, place the pan back over a gentle heat and allow to boil briefly – just a couple of lava-like bubbles are all you're looking for.

Pour into a shallow container and place a layer of cling film or a sprinkle of caster sugar over the surface to stop a skin forming.

GF

Chai custard

Difficulty: ◻ ◻
Makes: 380g custard

....

Prep: 20 mins
Infusing: 1 hr or
  overnight

....

1 x Vanilla Custard Base
  (see above)
1 cinnamon stick
5 green cardamom
  pods, bashed
5cm fresh ginger,
  peeled and sliced
  into 5mm coins

Infusing your cream and milk mixture with leaves, spices and herbs creates flavours that are only limited by your imagination! Use this custard in our Rhubarb and Ginger Crumble Danish Pastries (see page 200) and Apple and Raisin Chai Swirls (see page 191).

Follow the Vanilla Custard Base recipe (see above), adding the cinnamon, cardamom pods and ginger to the milk, cream and sugar mix (and omitting the vanilla). Warm the milk until lightly steaming, then remove from the heat and allow it to infuse for at least an hour, preferably overnight, in the fridge.

When you're ready to finish the custard, place the infused liquid (with the spices) into a pan to reheat until steaming, then strain (to remove the spices) over the egg/cornflour mix and continue as per the base recipe.

Bay custard

Difficulty: ⬚ ⬚
Makes: 380g custard

Prep: 20 mins
Infusing: 1 hr or
   overnight

1 x Vanilla Custard Base
   (see opposite)
10 fresh bay leaves

Use in our Poached Pear, Blackberry and Bay Danish Pastries (see page 199).

Follow the Vanilla Custard Base recipe (see opposite), crushing the bay leaves slightly in your hand before adding to the milk, cream, vanilla and sugar mix. Warm the milk until lightly steaming, then remove from the heat and allow to infuse for at least an hour, preferably overnight, in the fridge.

When you're ready to finish the custard, place the infused liquid (with the bay leaves) into a pan to reheat until steaming, then strain (to remove the leaves) over the egg/cornflour mix and continue as per the base recipe.

Fig leaf custard

Difficulty: ⬚ ⬚
Makes: 380g custard

Prep: 20 mins
Infusing: 1 hr or
   overnight

1 x Vanilla Custard Base
   (see opposite)
4 large fresh fig leaves

Use in our Honey, Fig and Sesame Danish Pastries (see page 203).

Follow the Vanilla Custard Base recipe (see opposite), toasting the fig leaves lightly under the grill until fragrant, then crushing slightly and adding them to the milk, cream, vanilla and sugar mix. Warm the milk until lightly steaming, then remove from the heat and allow to infuse for at least an hour, preferably overnight, in the fridge.

When you're ready to finish the custard, place the infused liquid (with the leaves) into a pan to reheat until steaming, then strain (to remove the leaves) over the egg/cornflour mix and continue as per the base recipe.

Vanilla custard (for doughnuts)

Difficulty: ⬚ ⬚
Fills: 10 doughnuts

Prep: 20 mins

1 x Vanilla Custard Base
   (see opposite)
75ml double cream

I spotted this crafty way of getting two types of custard for the price of one in the excellent *The Pastry Chef's Guide* by Ravneet Gill. Adding extra cream creates a silky, unctuous filling for doughnuts.

Follow the Vanilla Custard Base recipe (see opposite). Once thickened, place the pan back over a gentle heat and allow to boil briefly – just a couple of lava-like bubbles are all you're looking for. Stir in the cream to combine.

Pour into a shallow container and place a layer of cling film or a sprinkle of caster sugar over the surface to stop a skin forming.

Difficulty: ⛆ ⛆

Prep: 15 mins

Equipment: Digital
thermometer

120g caster sugar
60g egg whites
  (2 eggs), at room
  temperature

Italian meringue

This creates a stable meringue that's safe to eat uncooked with tall, satiny smooth peaks that can be shaped, sculpted and piped. The ratio of egg white to sugar is pretty much a constant for meringue, so scale up or down as required – one part egg white to two parts sugar.

Place the sugar in a small saucepan and add enough water to saturate. Heat over a high heat and as the water evaporates, the temperature will increase.

While the sugar is boiling, place the egg whites in the scrupulously clean bowl of your stand mixer or use electric beaters. Start whisking slowly – you want lots of small bubbles. Don't over-whisk/whisk too fast at this stage or the foam can collapse – it's more stable once the syrup is added.

When the sugar syrup reaches 116°C, reduce the speed to avoid splattering and pour the hot syrup over the whites. Increase the speed to full and whisk until the meringue has cooled and is thick, glossy and ready to pipe.

Meringue kisses

It's difficult to whisk small amounts of egg white so this makes plenty of kisses. Once cooled, they'll keep crisp in an airtight container indefinitely.

Preheat the oven to 140°C/120°C fan/gas 1. Cut baking parchment to the size of your baking sheet. Take a dab of meringue on your fingertip, apply to the four corners, then 'glue' your paper on top (to stop the paper lifting).

Spoon your cooled meringue into a piping bag with a 1.5cm round tip (or cut the tip off a disposable bag to the required size and twist the top). Don't fill the bag more than halfway full while you're learning. Hold the bag at the base (just behind the meringue) with your dominant hand – this is where you squeeze. Use the other hand to guide and stabilise the bag. Holding the bag in a vertical position over the sheet, start piping/squeezing just above the paper. Keep the pressure firm and smooth (not stop/start) and create the diameter you're after for the base of your kiss before you start lifting upwards. When your 'kiss' is big enough, gently lift the bag away in a vertical direction to create a point.

Continue to pipe, leaving a small space between each meringue kiss. Bake for 30–50 minutes until dry and hard. They should remain white throughout, so turn the sheet or reduce your oven temperature as required.

GF

Candied peel

Difficulty:

Prep: 20 mins
Cook: 1 hr
Dry: 1 hr

2 unwaxed oranges or lemons
200g caster sugar
20ml cold water

Wash the fruit, then peel the skin into thin strips using a vegetable peeler. Gather the strips together in small bunches and thinly slice the peel 1–2mm thick, using your fingers in the claw position (fingertips tucked in – knife against your knuckles).

Place the julienned peel into a pan of boiling water and simmer for 30 minutes. Once the peel has softened, drain and set aside.

Combine the sugar and cold water in the saucepan and bring to the boil before adding the rind into the sugar mixture. Reduce the heat and simmer gently for 20–25 minutes until the rinds are translucent.

Drain the rinds and place on baking parchment for a sticky peel or place on a lined baking tray in a low oven (120°C/100°C fan/gas ½) to dry for 1 hour. Store in an airtight container for up to 1 month.

GF

Nut and seed brittles

Difficulty:

Prep: 10 mins
Cook: 10 mins

100g whole or chopped nuts/seeds
200g caster sugar
Flaky sea salt

Brittles bring height, texture and colour to your bakes. Because caramel is hygroscopic (absorbs water from the air), it will start to get sticky and dissolve after a few hours in a moist environment, so add to your cakes and pastries just before serving.

Preheat the oven to 210°C/190°C fan/gas 6–7.

Place the nuts/seeds on a baking tray lined with baking parchment and roast them in the oven for 7–9 minutes until golden brown – the time will depend on their size, which will also dictate how thin your brittle can be.

In a small pan, add enough water to the sugar to saturate it, then place it over a medium heat. Caramelise to a golden colour, then pour over the nuts/seeds. Sprinkle over sea salt. Cool, then snap into shards. Store in a cool, dry place.

Difficulty: ⏲

Prep: 10 mins
Cook: 10 mins
Cool: 1–2 hrs

Equipment: Digital
 thermometer

225g caster sugar
110g golden syrup
10g bicarbonate of soda
1 tsp flaky sea salt

Honeycomb

Making a wet caramel is a bit like watching a snowball become an avalanche. You start out with a couple of innocuous ingredients boiling happily in a pan for what seems like ages and nothing much happens. Suddenly it reaches a tipping point (this is when all the water has boiled away) and everything speeds up very quickly – too quickly if you're not prepared! Add to this scenario the fact that you're dealing with hot liquid sugar that will burn your skin faster and more deeply than boiling water. Caramel isn't difficult but it does warrant respect and organisation.

Make sure everything you need for your caramel is prepared in advance and close to hand. Wear oven gloves. Put the plug in your sink and run some water – this will 'stop' your caramel if you place the pan's base into it.

Line a deep baking tray and place on a heatproof surface. The honeycomb will rise up alarmingly in the pan when you add the bicarbonate of soda and you will have to act quickly. Weigh out all your ingredients beforehand.

Place the sugar and golden syrup in a large, heavy-based pan and add enough water to saturate the sugar. Over a medium heat, let the sugar and syrup boil until it reaches 150°C – use a digital thermometer for accuracy.

When the sugar reaches 150°C, take the pan off the heat using an oven glove. Using a long-handled whisk, gently add the bicarbonate of soda into the caramel. It will foam up furiously – protect your face and hands.

Continue to stir the bubbling caramel for another 30 seconds, then pour it into the prepared tray. It will continue to darken for some minutes after it's poured into the tray, so remove it from the heat while it's still a pale golden colour. Sprinkle on the flaky sea salt. The caramel will stay very hot for some time – let the tray cool before attempting to move it.

When your honeycomb is cold, tip it out of the tray and, using a rolling pin, break it into big chunks or make Salted Honeycomb Crunch (see below).

Salted honeycomb crunch

Place some honeycomb into a bowl with a pinch of sea salt crystals and bash together using the end of a rolling pin until the desired level of crumbs is achieved. Delicious on your doughnuts, ice cream or as a cake topping.

GF

Salted caramel sauce

Difficulty: ○

Prep: 5 mins
Cook: 20 mins

200g caster sugar
70g unsalted butter,
  chopped into cubes
1 tsp vanilla extract
120ml double cream
1 tsp flaky sea salt

> **BAKER'S TIP**
>
> To clean your caramel pan, run hot water into the pan and leave it for a few minutes to dissolve the caramel. No elbow grease involved!

Put a small plate in the fridge to chill, then clean a large jam jar and place in the oven at 120°C/100°C fan/gas ½ to sterilise.

Place the sugar in a medium, heavy-based pan and add enough water to saturate the sugar. Over a low heat, let the sugar caramelise until it turns a deep amber colour, stirring occasionally to incorporate and dissolve all the sugar – this could take between 5 and 10 minutes.

While the sugar caramelises, weigh the butter and add the vanilla to the cream – you need to add it to the pan as soon as it reaches the right colour.

When the sugar is ready, remove from the heat and carefully stir in the butter followed by the cream – take care as the caramel will boil up and splatter. Finally, stir in the salt.

Return to the heat and bring to the boil again until the caramel reaches the level of thickness required – check by dripping a little onto the cold plate. As it cools, push the caramel with a finger to see if it wrinkles, remembering that the caramel will firm up as it cools. Pour into the warmed jar, add the lid, cool and store in the fridge, warming it before use.

GF

Stock syrup

Difficulty: ○

Prep: 5 mins
Cook: 10 mins

300g caster sugar
300ml water
2 star anise
1 cinnamon stick
5 cloves

A stock syrup is useful for brushing onto the cut surface of cakes to keep them moist. This simple recipe is a pastry chef's best-kept secret! You can tweak the flavours of the base recipe, adding/removing different spices or adding a splash of rum or brandy.

Place the sugar and water in a small pan with the spices. Bring to a simmer and stir until the sugar is fully dissolved. Pour into a heatproof container with a lid. Cool and store in the fridge. This will keep for up to a month.

Chocolate tempering

Difficulty: ⏻ ⏻ ⏻

....

Process: 30 minutes

....

**Equipment: Digital
thermometer**

Slowly heating and cooling melted chocolate helps cocoa butter fats to crystallise uniformly – known as tempering. Tempered chocolate has a smooth, glossy finish and a good snap. Chocolate that is not tempered properly melts quickly, has a crumbly texture and a dull and streaky surface. This isn't the simplest process, but it's incredibly satisfying once you've mastered it. You can keep practising with the same chocolate – melting and seeding it again and again.

Place 5cm of water in a small pan and heat until simmering. Place a heatproof bowl on top of the pan, without touching the water below. Chop your chocolate into small, even pieces, then place three-quarters into the bowl (e.g. 300g if you're wanting to temper 400g in total), reserving the rest for later. Melt, stirring occasionally. Make sure no steam or moisture gets into the bowl. Dark chocolate will melt at 50–55°C and white and milk chocolate will melt at 40–45°C.

Once melted, remove the bowl from the heat and gradually stir in the reserved chocolate – this is called seeding. The temperature should now be around 27/28°C for dark chocolate or 25/26°C for milk or white chocolate.

Place the bowl back on top of the simmering water and stir continually while the temperature rises to 31/32°C for dark chocolate, 29°C for milk chocolate or 28°C for white chocolate.

To test if your chocolate is tempered, spread a thin layer onto a cold plate with a palette knife. Tempered chocolate will set very quickly to a shiny, smooth finish. Stir well and use immediately.

Chocolate bark

We like to flavour tempered chocolate by sprinkling toppings onto the surface. Once the chocolate has gone hard, snap it into shards for decorating cakes or package it up prettily to give as gifts.

Follow the method for chocolate tempering (see above), then pour your tempered chocolate onto a piece of baking parchment and use a palette knife or spatula to smooth it out. Sprinkle on your choice of nuts, seeds or freeze-dried fruit while the chocolate is still liquid. Set at room temperature.

Sourdough culture

The only skills required to create your culture are a regular feeding routine (the culture – not you) and patience. You'll also need a clear cylindrical container (tall and narrow is best), weighing scales, rye or stoneground wholemeal flour, strong white bread flour, a rubber band or marker pen and a notebook.

1. Lots of tiny bubbles on the surface mean your culture needs a feed.

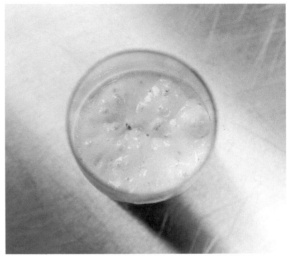

2. This shows a healthy starter – thick with big bubbles.

3. This is a mouldy starter just out of the fridge. It's not dead but just needs discard/feeding over a few days.

4. Your culture is ready to use when it's doubled in volume but hasn't started to slide back to where it started.

Create a flour feeding mix

Before you start, mix equal amounts of either rye or wholemeal flour with your strong white bread flour and store in a container to use as your 'base flour mix'. It makes things quicker as you won't need to find multiple bags of flour each day.

STAGE 1

| DAY 1 | In your clear container, combine 50g of warm water with 50g of your flour mix (100g total) to make a thick, gloopy paste (this will now be referred to as your culture). Clean down the sides with the back of a spoon, creating a level surface, and put a rubber band around this line or mark with a pen. Cover loosely, then place somewhere consistently warm – your oven with just the light on or an airing cupboard that doesn't get too hot will give you that sweet spot of 26°C. |

| DAY 2 | Don't feed or discard your culture – just keep it warm and let those microorganisms start feeding and making friends. |

| DAY 3 | Discard 50g of your culture and then combine what's left with 50g of the flour mix and 50g of warm water (total 150g). |

| DAY 4 | Discard 100g of your culture and then combine what's left with 50g of the flour mix and 50g of warm water (total 150g). |

| DAY 5 | Discard 100g of your culture and then combine what's left with 50g of the flour mix and 50g of warm water (total 150g). |

| DAY 6 | Discard 100g of your culture and then combine what's left with 50g of the flour mix and 50g of warm water (total 150g). |

| DAY 7 | Discard 100g of your culture and then combine what's left with 50g of the flour mix and 50g of warm water (total 150g). |

Each day, at feeding time, look closely at what's going on in your jar and write down any changes. Check how much the culture has risen (use your rubber band or pen marker to help you), changes in the smell and gas activity (look at the bottom of the jar). Around day 8 you'll hopefully see that your culture is doubling in size between feeds, or it may already have peaked and be sliding back down the jar. These are signs that you're ready to move on to Stage 2. This may happen sooner or later than day 8, so adapt accordingly.

As the yeasts and bacteria respond to daily feeding, they'll become increasingly active, multiply in number and the carbon dioxide gas they're producing will become trapped in the gluten network, pushing the culture upwards in the jar. As fermentation begins, flavours and smells go from odourless and floury to yoghurty-sweet and then sharp and alcoholic – taste it as part of your daily observation. These stronger smells occur when the microorganisms run out of food and begin producing acetic acid and ethanol – a sure sign that you're ready to move the feeding ratio to less culture and more food. It'll be approximately 1 part culture to 5 parts flour mix/5 parts water by the time it's ready to start baking with it.

STAGE 2		
	DAY 8	Discard 120g of your culture and combine what's left (30g) with 50g of the flour mix and 50g of warm water (total 130g).
	DAY 9	Discard 110g of your culture and combine what's left (20g) with 50g of the flour mix and 50g of warm water (total 120g).
	DAY 10	Discard 110g of your culture and combine what's left (10g) with 45g of the flour mix and 45g of warm water (total 100g).

Maintaining and building your sourdough culture

Your culture should now be ready to use, though you may need to make a bit more for your recipe. See 'Your schedule for success' on page 132. If you're baking several times a week, you can leave your culture ambient in your kitchen, discarding and feeding it every 24 hours. If you're baking less than twice a week, it's much easier to keep it in your fridge but be sure to re-awaken it with food and warmth at least 2–3 days before baking.

Treat it with love – it's part of your family. Once you get to know its ways, you'll be rewarded with delicious bread for years and years to come.

Glossary

Yeasts

Baker's yeast (*Saccharomyces cerevisiae*)

Baker's yeast is a commercially cultivated, single-celled microorganism that gives consistent results. In warm, moist environments (i.e. the 26°C dough you've created) the yeast uses enzymes to break down the simple sugars in flour to provide it with food. As it feeds, the yeast cells respire, producing carbon dioxide that expands the network of gluten proteins, making the bread rise. Yeast is available in both fresh and dry forms. Neither type is 'better' or 'worse'. Just remember that dried yeast is more concentrated, so use half the amount in a recipe asking for fresh yeast.

Baker's yeast (in contrast to sourdough) has got a bit of a bad reputation in recent years due to industrial processes (I'm looking at you, Chorleywood process) that use large quantities of yeast to make bread very quickly by intensively mixing and heating their dough. This bread lacks taste and texture and can be indigestible to parts of the population. In contrast, making bread slowly by proving it over several hours, or even days, requires very small amounts of yeast (relative to flour weight) and produces bread with great flavour and nutritional qualities – just how we like it.

Wild yeast (also known as sourdough yeast culture)

A combination of wild yeasts and bacteria, co-existing in a slurry of flour and water. Wild yeasts are present in the air that we breathe and the grains that we bake with. Lactic acid bacteria (LAB) are commonly present on rotting fruit and vegetables and even on our own skin. Once introduced to flour, warmth and moisture, the yeasts produce carbon dioxide gas that slowly expands the network of gluten proteins, causing the dough to rise. At the same time, lactic acid bacteria produce lactic acid, acetic acid and ethanol, while lowering the pH of the dough and starting a chain reaction of sugar and starch consumption that enhances the flavour, aroma and texture of the developing dough.

Flours

Choosing flour for your next project is a serious business. I've lost whole days standing in the home-baking aisle of a well-stocked supermarket contemplating the different grains, grists and blends, searching for enlightenment in the small print.

Understanding different flours helps you create the type of bread you and your family want to eat – whether it's white and chewy or dense and wholesome. When you're shopping around for flour, don't just limit yourself to the supermarket – Britain has seen an exponential rise in the numbers of small farm producers and millers exploring the potential of different varieties of grains. If you're new to baking bread, I'd encourage you to stick with one flour for at least three bakes, while you develop an understanding of its properties and flavour. My experience is that American flours absorb water differently from English milled wheats. Adapt your water quantity accordingly.

How grain becomes flour

Flour is produced from a variety of cereal crops, wheat being the most common in this country. At harvest time, the grain is stripped from the stalk, separated from its outer husk, then stoneground or roller-milled to produce the powdery substance we know as flour.

Stoneground

Using two mill stones, traditionally powered by water, the whole grain is ground down to create delicious flour that takes longer to digest because of the larger particles of fibrous husk and nutritious wheatgerm.

Roller-milled

Most of the flour we consume today is roller-milled for efficiency and speed of processing. The process extracts as much of the white endosperm as possible to produce a pure white flour. Ironically, modern milling methods remove the parts of the grain that are most important to our health (wheatgerm and high fibre-bran) and by law the miller is required to replace the missing nutrients.

Grains

Wheat (*Triticum aestivum*)

Working with wheat flour is a good place to start – gluten development, water absorbency and dough handling is more straightforward, making it easier to identify the different stages of fermentation. The strength of wheat flour refers to glutenin and gliadin protein levels in the grain. When wheat flour is mixed with liquid, the two proteins join to form gluten. Hard wheat varieties create flours of 10–14% protein, suitable for breadmaking and labelled 'strong' or 'very strong'. Bread dough needs a chewy, elastic texture and requires high protein flours. In cakes and pastry, where a delicate, tender crumb is required, mixing is minimised. These flours are described as 'plain', 'soft' or 'all-purpose' and have a lower protein level (7–8g per 100g of flour). You can combine flours with different protein levels to good effect. Our East Coast Rye (see page 142) uses a strong wheat flour to prop up the weak rye flour, while in our Spiced Double Chocolate Cookies (see page 62) we've replaced some of the weak plain flour with bread flour for a chewier cookie.

Spelt (*Triticum spelta*)

Another early cultivar of modern wheat, originally cultivated in Iran and southwest Europe and still widely used in Swiss and German breads. It has a nutty flavour and is higher in the protein gliadin than glutenin, which makes gluten development more fragile. Vigorous kneading and mixing should be avoided.

Rye (*Secale cereale*)

First cultivated around 400BC, this nutrient-packed flour is important in Eastern European and Scandinavian baking as it grows well in cold, wet climates. Usually unrefined, instead of elastic gluten, rye contains a starch called pentosan, which acts like glue, trapping water molecules and creating a dense, sticky dough. Warm water activates rye's enzymes and complex carbohydrates and encourages higher acetic acid production, creating flavour. Rye flour produces a dark, sour, dense loaf that keeps for months rather than days because it can absorb and retain moisture.

Milling and blending

Extraction rate

This is the percentage of whole grain that remains after milling. The higher the extraction rate, the more bran and germ are left in the flour. Higher extraction flours absorb more water because of the large particles of bran, so adapt accordingly.

White flour

Made from the soft, powdery inner part of the grain known as the endosperm, white flour has an extraction rate of 70–75%. High in carbohydrates and calories, it must be fortified by law because essential nutrients such as iron and calcium are removed during milling. Protein levels vary depending on the wheat variety and how close the flour is to the outer husk of the grain.

Wholemeal flour

This flour is 100% extraction because it contains the whole grain (endosperm, germ and bran). High in protein, fibre, unsaturated fats, amino acids and omega-3 oils, the term can be applied to all the grains e.g. spelt, rye, etc. Despite wholemeal flours being strong due to their protein content, they need longer to fully hydrate the bran and the dough needs gentle handling to minimise the damaging effect of bran on developing gluten. Stoneground wholemeal flour usually has larger particles of bran and germ than roller-milled, which creates a heavier, denser loaf. The higher fat content of wholemeal flour makes it more perishable than white. Keep in a cool place and use within 3 months.

Water (hydration)

Water makes up a significant proportion of your dough, sometimes almost as much as the flour weight. The wetter your dough, the faster it will ferment and the more open your crumb will be. Tap water is perfectly fine to use for breadmaking, though very hard water can slow fermentation down slightly.

The term hydration refers to the weight of water in your dough relative to flour weight. Using bakers' percentages, flour is always 100% and water is a percentage of that weight. For example, if your recipe asks for 1kg of flour and 700g of water, then the hydration rate would be 70%. Some flours can be thirstier than others (the bran in wholemeal flour makes it more absorbent), so bear this in mind when working with a new flour and be prepared to adjust your water accordingly.

Salt

Salt causes flour molecules to attach more strongly to each other, forming long-chain proteins that tighten the dough as the gluten matrix strengthens. Salt attracts moisture, so slows down fermentation and affects the ability of flour to hydrate properly. I use fine sea salt as it contains nothing but salt.

Acknowledgements

From the three people baking on opening day to a small army today, we've been lucky enough to have worked alongside many knowledgeable bakers and chefs, all of whom share our ethos and care passionately about their craft. Their skills haven't been forgotten or taken for granted and many, past and present, feature in this book. Their differing strengths and talents have contributed to, and shaped, Two Magpies – making us the business we are today.

Thank you to 'Team Magpies' past and present – the business (and this book) represents a little bit of everyone that has ever worked for us or whose path I have been lucky enough to have crossed during my reincarnation as a baker. Your differing strengths, talents and passions have contributed to, and shaped us, making us what we are today.

Thanks to Sam Cutter and Aimee Roberts, our first two bakers and graduates of the School of Artisan Food, who implemented many of the methods and systems we still have in place today. Special thanks to David Nizi, baker extraordinaire, for his generosity, support and baking inspiration. Thanks for the help and support, especially during those difficult times, of Wayne Caddy, Richard and Kate from Holtwhites Bakery and especially Martha Brown at Forge Bakehouse. To Chris Young from the Real Bread Campaign for believing in me as a baker even when I didn't really believe in myself.

Thanks to Michelle Wade and Ashton Lee for helping create such beautiful bakes for the photoshoot. Thanks to Fern Harman and Guy Watts for developing and sharing some of the recipes in this book and to all the other bakers whose paths I've crossed who have generously shared their ideas and knowledge.

Thanks to Steve Magnall, my business partner, for giving me the time to finally finish writing this book – it's only taken 7 years!

Thanks to my children Faith, Jimmy and Betsy for their endless positivity and encouragement and for putting up with some pretty terrible bread and cakes while I was learning. I wouldn't be writing these words without your support. Thanks to my parents John and Barbara Harrison for being there for me.

Thanks to India Hobson and Magnus Edmondson. You are both an inspiration and a joy to work with. Thanks to Emma Lahaye for working her magic during the photoshoot and for supplying such endless patience, wonderful ideas and amazing crockery!

Thanks to John Bond who started the ball rolling, which led me to my editor Anna Steadman who listened and encouraged. The ball then continued to the author Jane Lovett who was generous enough to listen and put me in touch with my lovely agent Heather Holden-Brown. Thanks to Kay Halsey for her patience and attention to detail and to Nathan Burton for making the book come alive so beautifully.

And lastly, a huge thanks to the many loyal customers who've cheered us on and buoyed us up along the way – we certainly couldn't have done it without you!

'Two Magpies Bakery is the greatest
thing to happen to Suffolk this decade.
Rebecca and her team make the
greatest bread, the most wholesome
but imaginative cakes and have a
mission to use local ingredients that
inspire game-changing results. Hers is
the only shop I will happily queue in. And
I'll be doing the same at the bookshop
when her recipes are finally published.'

EMMA FREUD

STOCKISTS

Marriage's – millers of wonderful flour

Hodmedod's – Suffolk-based producers
of pulses and grains

BakeryBits – online bakery ingredients
and equipment

Rackmaster – specialist trays and tins

Fen Farm Dairy – lovely people making
delicious cheese

Allpress Coffee – this New Zealand coffee
brand has been with us from the start

Adnams – flavourful beers and a Southwold
institution!

Photography © 2023 India Hobson

First published in 2023 by Headline Home
an imprint of Headline Publishing Group

2

Cataloguing in Publication Data is available from the British Library

ISBN 9781472295903
eBook ISBN 9781472295910

Commissioning Editor: Anna Steadman
Senior Editor: Kate Miles
Project Editor: Kay Halsey
Design: Nathan Burton
Publicity: Alara Delfosse and Isabelle Wilson
Marketing: Lucy Hall
Photography: India Hobson and Magnus Edmondson
Food and Prop Styling: Emma Lahaye
Proofreader: Anne Sheasby and Vicky Orchard
Indexer: Ruth Ellis

Colour reproduction by Alta Image
Printed and bound in China by C&C Offset Printing Co., Ltd

HEADLINE PUBLISHING GROUP
An Hachette UK Company
Carmelite House
50 Victoria Embankment
London EC4Y 0DZ

www.headline.co.uk
www.hachette.co.uk